Community and Conflict

Community and Conflict

The Sources of Liberal Solidarity

Derek Edyvane

First published 2007 by
PALGRAVE MACMILLAN
Houndmills, Basingstoke, Hampshire RG21 6XS and
175 Fifth Avenue, New York, N. Y. 10010
Companies and representatives throughout the world

PALGRAVE MACMILLAN is the global academic imprint of the Palgrave Macmillan division of St. Martin's Press, LLC and of Palgrave Macmillan Ltd. Macmillan® is a registered trademark in the United States, United Kingdom and other countries. Palgrave is a registered trademark in the European Union and other countries.

ISBN-13: 978–0–230–50686–2   hardback
ISBN-10: 0–230–50686–0   hardback

This book is printed on paper suitable for recycling and made from fully managed and sustained forest sources. Logging, pulping and manufacturing processes are expected to conform to the environmental regulations of the country of origin.

A catalogue record for this book is available from the British Library.

Library of Congress Cataloging-in-Publication Data
Edyvane, Derek, 1977–
    Community and conflict : the sources of liberal solidarity / Derek Edyvane.
        p. cm.
    Includes bibliographical references and index.
    ISBN 0–230–50686–0 (cloth)
    1. Communities. 2. Communities–Political aspects. 3. Communities in literature. 4. Social conflict. 5. Solidarity. I. Title.

    HM756.E39 2007
    307.01'4–dc22   2006048882

10   9   8   7   6   5   4   3   2   1
16   15   14   13   12   11   10   09   08   07

Printed and bound in Great Britain by
Antony Rowe Ltd, Chippenham and Eastbourne

For Alison and John

Contents

Acknowledgements

The vast majority of this book was written in 2006 during a period of postdoctoral research, kindly funded by the British Academy. The British Academy postdoctoral fellowship has provided me with essential financial support without which this book may never have been written, and it also provided me three very enjoyable years in which I have had the luxury of being able to devote myself full-time to the pursuit of my research interests. I am extremely grateful for having been afforded this opportunity.

The project as whole has occupied me for a far longer period of time, however, and I have incurred numerous debts along the way. I have spent the last eight years based in the department of politics at the University of York, first as an MA student during which time I received financial support from the J.B. Morrell Trust, then as a PhD student generously funded by the Arts and Humanities Research Board and finally as a British Academy postdoctoral fellow. I would like to express my thanks to the University and particularly to the staff and students of the department of politics for providing the necessary institutional support and a very rich, stimulating and friendly research culture. I do not doubt that the absence of such a hospitable environment would have made these last years a vastly more difficult and lonely time.

Connectedly, I would like to express my gratitude to all of those friends and colleagues who have listened to my ideas or otherwise kept me sane over the years. In particular, I am grateful to Rob Wavre, Sarah Oester, Rebecca Dickenson, Sarah Marshall, Sam Clark, Emily Clark, Chris Hallam, Alex Shaw, Paul Thomas, Eduardo Dargent, Matt Sleat, Tim Stanton, Jon Parkin and Alex Bavister-Gould. I have learned an enormous amount from all of them. I am especially grateful to those who played a direct role in supporting my research. I would like to express my warmest thanks to Matt Matravers who served as my back-up supervisor on the PhD, to Peter Nicholson who served as my temporary supervisor (during spring, 2000), and to Andrew Mason who acted as my PhD external examiner. I would also like to thank the undergraduate students who participated in the 'Community and Freedom' module, which I taught in the summer term of 2006, for helping me to road test many of the ideas that appear in this book. My thanks go also to Dan Bunyard at Palgrave for seeing me through the publishing process and to the anonymous reviewer who offered very extensive and helpful comments on the book proposal.

There are four people to whom I am particularly indebted. First, I would like to express my deepest gratitude to Sue Mendus. She has served both as my PhD supervisor and as my mentor for the post-doctoral fellowship. She has read and provided detailed and insightful comments on almost everything I have written over the last eight years, including this book, and she has given generously of her time throughout. She has been an abiding source of academic and personal support. My debt to her is thus considerable. I would also like to offer my heartfelt thanks to Valeria Guarneros who has admirably tolerated and consoled me, even at my most intolerable and inconsolable during the research process. She is my good companion. Finally, I offer my thanks to my parents, Alison and John. Their support has been unparalleled and invaluable from start to finish. I dedicate this book to them.

Derek Edyvane, July 2006

Introduction: Strangers

> Modern society is indeed often, at least in surface appearance, nothing but a collection of strangers, each pursuing his or her own interests under minimal constraints. (Alasdair MacIntyre, 1985, 250–1)

We have a very deep belief that the bond of community must be understood primarily in terms of agreement about morality and the good life. As Chandran Kukathas writes, 'it is the understandings people share that make them into a community' (Kukathas, 2003, 170). Disagreements and the conflicts they inspire, by contrast, are thought to be destructive of the possibility of community. Where we lack a shared conception of morality and the good life, we are liable to be as the strangers MacIntyre portrays: each pursuing his or her own interests with no non-instrumental regard for others. In this book, I shall argue that this belief is false. Conflict is no barrier to community. On the contrary, disagreement and mutual disapproval may even serve to provide important routes into political association with one's fellow citizens.

In order to sharpen the focus here, I shall open with a puzzle. In *After Virtue*, Alasdair MacIntyre articulates a pretty desolate vision of modern life neatly digested in the quotation with which I began. We moderns live in a world 'after virtue'. Our moral beliefs are necessarily incoherent because we no longer share an authoritative conception of the good life from which a meaningful morality could plausibly derive its force. And so we are as strangers to one another. Having nothing in common, we each pursue our individual purposes

1

under the minimal constraints of a modern liberal democracy. This reflects an immensely powerful and influential vision of modern life as an existence in which, to misquote Marx, 'all that was solid has melted into air'. The old moral certainties are gone and we are at sea in a society devoid of solidarity and communal warmth. We are lost, both to one another and increasingly to ourselves.

The assertion that we are strangers in MacIntyre's sense has received considerable support in the sociological literature. The research of Robert Putnam identifies a sharp decline of what he terms 'social capital' in American society since around the mid-1960s (Putnam, 2000).[1] Social capital, he explains, 'refers to connections among individuals – social networks and the norms of reciprocity and trustworthiness that arise from them' (Putnam, 2000, 19). He demonstrates that following a peak in the 1960s, the membership of Americans in civic associations has fallen fairly steadily across the board (Putnam, 2000, 48–64). As he puts it: 'Americans have been dropping out in droves, not merely from political life, but from organized community life more generally' (Putnam, 2000, 63). And this decline in citizen participation has coincided with a fall in altruism, volunteering and philanthropy. Putnam observes that total charitable giving has fallen as a fraction of national income from 2.26 percent in 1964 to 1.61 percent in 1998, a relative fall of 29 percent (Putnam, 2000, 123). Americans have also become less trusting. Putnam reports that 'at century's end, a generation with a trust quotient of nearly 80 percent was being rapidly replaced by one with a trust quotient of barely half that' (Putnam, 2000, 141).[2]

Further support for MacIntyre's contention can be found in the research of Robert Bellah and his assistants, assembled in their *Habits of the Heart*. Based on fieldwork conducted between 1979 and 1984, and involving interviews with over 200 'middle Americans', the researchers sought to uncover 'what resources Americans have for making sense of their lives, how they think about themselves and their society, and how their ideas relate to their actions' (Bellah *et al.*, 1985, x). The central thesis, which runs right through the work, is as follows:

[America] is a society in which the individual can only rarely and with difficulty understand himself and his activities as interrelated in morally meaningful ways with those of other, different Americans. Instead of directing cultural and individual energies to relating the self to its larger context, the culture ... urges a strenuous effort to make of our particular segment of life a small world of its own (Bellah *et al.*, 1985, 50).

The research suggests that Americans are increasingly driven into 'lifestyle enclaves' – private associations with those who share a conception of the good life – for at the level of the society, there is no sense of belonging. As one individual remarked, 'Many people feel empty and don't know why they feel empty ... Loneliness is a national feeling' (Bellah *et al.*, 1985, 158).

Many interviewees drew a sharp distinction between an idealized vision of the local and consensual politics of the community (or the lifestyle enclave) on the one hand, and a rather less favourable conception of what is termed the 'politics of interest' on the other (Bellah *et al.*, 1985, 199). And they conclude that Americans 'feel most comfortable in thinking about politics in terms of a consensual community of autonomous, but essentially similar individuals. ... For all the lip service given to respect for cultural differences, Americans seem to lack the resources to think about the relationship between groups that are culturally, socially or economically quite different' (Bellah *et al.*, 1985, 206). The researchers conclude that Americans have difficulty identifying with other members of their society where those others hold conceptions of the good different from their own. This, in turn, encourages them to regard political interaction with their fellow citizens as a rather unpalatable activity.

So there is much to be said in favour of MacIntyre's characterization of modern democratic society as a collection of strangers. Nevertheless, it seems that in the stark form in which MacIntyre presents it, his claim must be false. This is the puzzle: even in surface appearance, it is just not true that modern society resembles nothing more than a collection of self-interested atoms. Our everyday lives reveal a number of very well established practices which render the charge of estrangement incredibly difficult to sustain, at least in its strongest form. It would be hard to deny that estrangement plays a part in modern life, but I want to develop a more complex picture of modernity as colourful in its chaos, essential in its terror; an environment in which we feel at ease partly because it is disjointed, fluid and conflicted. I am going to explain what I mean here in rather more detail than may presently seem necessary. For reasons that will become clearer as we proceed, an awareness of these practices is very important to the larger strategy of the book, so I think it is worth spelling them out carefully at this early stage.

Whilst I would not wish to dispute Putnam's claim that our 'trust quotient' is plummeting, I think it important not to ignore the deep and remarkably stable networks of trust that underpin the whole of modern life. As Martin Hollis has observed, without trust, 'social life would be impossible' (Hollis, 1998, 1). It seems to me that this is an important insight far too readily overlooked – and quite possibly overlooked by the respondents in Putnam's survey. Hollis provides some indication of this:

> Everyday life is a catalogue of success in the exercise of trust. Our dealings with friends and enemies, neighbours and strangers depend on it, whether in homes, streets, markets, seats of government or other arenas of civil society. Would you ask a stranger the time unless you could normally count on a true answer? Could you use the highway without trusting other drivers? Could an economy progress beyond barter, or a society beyond mud huts unless people relied on one another to keep their promises? (Hollis, 1998, 1)

Every day, over and over again, we unhesitatingly place ourselves into the hands of our fellow citizens. As Annette Baier observes, we 'trust those we encounter in lonely library stacks to be searching for books, not victims. We sometimes let ourselves fall asleep on trains and planes, trusting neighboring strangers not to take advantage of our defencelessness. We put our bodily safety into the hands of pilots, drivers, and doctors with scarcely any sense of recklessness' (Baier, 1994, 98). All of this is very easy to miss simply because we have become so accustomed to seeing our trust rewarded as those upon whom we rely behave, time and time again, exactly as expected: we 'inhabit a climate of trust as we inhabit an atmosphere and notice it as we notice air, only when it becomes scarce or polluted' (Baier, 1994, 98). We are so accustomed to the practice of trust that we scarcely notice just how remarkable it actually is. On the whole, we are willing to trust our fellow citizens and we are very often willing to trust them with our lives; and, what is more, we are so confident of their trustworthiness that we very rarely even notice the extent of our dependence upon them.

Perhaps it would be a mistake to read too much into the prevalence of trust in our lives. Daniel Weinstock writes that it seems 'sufficient for the trust I vest in the total stranger on the street from whom I ask directions to be justified that he not have any positive reason to steer me wrong. It seems odd to say that he must be positively well-disposed toward me, or that his motivations toward me be benevolent, as a condition of meriting my trust' (Weinstock, 1999, 293). Nevertheless, the bond of trust certainly sits very uneasily with the idea that our relations with our fellow citizens can be adequately captured in entirely instrumental terms. The ubiquity of trust in modern societies reveals our broader tendency to sociality. It reveals something of the respect we generally have for one another. As Weinstock argues, 'the action of placing one's trust in others expresses one's belief that the other is *capable* of acting in a manner respectful of the personhood of others' (Weinstock, 1999, 295). Trust also reveals the extent of our dependence upon one another. After all, why do we so often find it necessary to trust those around us? Baier argues that it is because we need each other, because the things we typically value 'include things that we cannot single-handedly either create or sustain (our own life, health, reputation, our off-spring and their well-being, as well as intrinsically shared goods such as conversation, its written equivalent, theater and other forms of play, chamber music, market exchange, political life, and so on)' (Baier, 1994, 101). The fact that trust is such a pronounced feature of our lives reveals that mutual dependence and the measure of respect it implies are widespread.

It might be said that we only trust our fellow citizens because it pays to do so: we would struggle to pursue our private interests, indeed we would struggle to survive at all, if we could not rely on others in certain contexts. But this is problematic, for clearly trusting does not always pay. Even if we tilt the balance with the imposition of various penalties on untrustworthy behaviour, it seems that there will always be occasions on which the pursuit of my private interests dictates dishonesty. As Hollis observes, granted 'that policing, informal and formal alike, is both costly and inefficient, trust is too vulnerable to free-riders' (Hollis, 1998, 32). In any case, it just seems rather too grim and cynical a view of modern life to hold that we are trustworthy only because and in so far as it is in our self-interest to be so given that we fear the consequences of free-riding. It just rings false. To be sure, such an explanation is probably true of *some* people. Some people can be trusted only because of the CCTV cameras tracking their every movement. But equally, it is not at all absurd to suppose that the bond of trust is very often effective just because we are genuinely respectful of one another.

Weinstock may be right to suggest that successful instances of trust need not be thought to imply any sort of positive concern between the involved parties, but we do in fact very often display positive concern for our fellow citizens. Often this occurs in very small ways: we hold doors open for strangers, we help people to pick up the things they have dropped, we smile at one another and say hello, we give up our seats on public transport for those who need them more than we do. Small kindnesses like these are the stuff of everyday life and there are myriads of examples with which we are all extremely familiar. Indeed, it seems to me that we may say here much the same as we said of trust. The expression of kindness is so commonplace, so much a feature of our ordinary experience that we tend not to notice just how prevalent it is. Like trust, we inhabit a climate of kindness as we inhabit an atmosphere and notice it as we notice air, only when it becomes scarce or polluted. It is also worth noting that very often such acts of kindness are not perceived as acts of charity or munificence; they are more closely identified with duty. Of course it would be nice of me to give up my seat on the bus for the elderly gentleman, but it seems a mistake to think that by moving I would be acting charitably. While the term 'duty' itself might have the wrong connotations here, given that it is often contrasted with the ideas of 'concern' or 'kindness', we do think that to move in such circumstances constitutes some kind of obligation, a form of common decency expected of any person who is genuinely concerned for those around them. In other words, such acts of kindness are typically regarded as expressions of genuine concern. We *are* genuinely concerned for our fellow citizens and you can see it reflected in the innumerable kindnesses that punctuate our daily lives.

And it is not only in our face-to-face encounters that the practice of mutual concern is in evidence. Concern is apparent on a much larger, political, scale mediated by the institutions of the welfare state (as partial and fragile as it has become). Michael Ignatieff argues that the redistribution of wealth 'through the numberless capillaries of the state' from rich to poor, independent to dependent, serves to 'establish a silent relation between' the strangers of a liberal society (Ignatieff, 1984, 10). Of course some people begrudge the fact that their earnings are diverted to pay for the education, healthcare and general well-being of their fellow citizens, but many do not. Many people think it important that wealth be redistributed to at least some degree. Many of us regard this again as an expression of genuine concern.

A particularly striking instance of the practice of concern that I am trying to articulate here is provided by the case of blood donation. Once again, I do not wish to dispute Putnam's observation that blood donation has declined. I am sure that this is true, but what is much more remarkable is the fact that people continue to give blood at all. If we were really nothing but self-interested strangers, then we would expect those Richard Titmuss has labelled 'voluntary community donors', who donate their blood as a free gift to anonymous others, not to exist in our society. But they clearly do. Voluntary community donors are distinguishable by the fact that they receive no reward of any kind for their donations; they pay no penalty of any kind for failing to donate; and they donate in the absence of any knowledge about the recipient of the blood (Titmuss, 1970, 89). Blood donation denotes a non-contractual, gift-relationship between those who donate and those who receive.

It is thus rather difficult to reconcile this image of the voluntary community donor with the mutually unconcerned collection of strangers we are supposed to have become. I suppose there are ways of reconciling them: undergraduate students have been known to insist that they donate blood simply because it allows them to get drunk more cheaply following the donation. More seriously, it is not unheard of for people to donate blood because they would like to gather information about it for the sake of their own health. But if one examines the reasons people give for donating blood, it becomes apparent that they rarely cast their motivation in such individualistic or self-interested terms. Titmuss reports a considerable variety of different responses to the question 'Could you say why you *first* decided to become a blood donor' (Titmuss, 1970,

226–36)?[3] The most common response was that 'I might need blood myself one day'. On the face of it, this seems an entirely individual-istic and self-interested answer, but as Martin Hollis has argued, appearances here may be deceiving, for the response makes 'no rational "economic" sense'. 'The blood I give today will not be restored to me if I need some next year, nor does my giving it make it significantly likelier that there will be enough blood for me then. My gift puts me no higher in the queue if supplies are short' (Hollis, 1998, 145). The point is that strangers each pursuing their own interests under minimal constraints have little or no reason to donate blood. Consequently, Hollis concludes that 'unless the respondents were simply stupid, the reply that "I might need blood myself one day" was a cover for a non-economic motive which they did not care to voice' (Hollis, 1998, 146).

Hollis suggests that the 'underlying motive presumably surfaced in the next most common replies' which were broadly altruistic in form and were presented in an ethical vocabulary (Hollis, 1998, 146). One person gave blood from 'a desire to help other people in need'; another suggested that 'no man is an island'. In summary, nearly 80 percent of the answers given implied 'a high sense of social responsibility towards the needs of other members of society' (Titmuss, 1970, 236). Of course, we could speculate endlessly about the sincerity of these responses, but there seems to be very little reason to take them at anything other than their face value. People often donate blood just because they are genuinely concerned for those around them, whoever they may be.

Another way of interpreting MacIntyre's sociological claim is that we are strangers in the sense that we have and want nothing to do with one another. We are alienated and dislocated like the Americans portrayed by Bellah and his assistants. But again this seems a very partial account. Consider the life of any modern (democratic) city. They are full of public spaces that we willingly and enthusiastically share with strangers: bars, cafes, pubs, parks, museums, galleries, theatres, libraries. We could easily confine our-selves to the familiarity of our respective 'lifestyle enclaves', but so often we do exactly the opposite and venture out into the public space yearning to be where the action is. Consider, for example, Iris Marion Young's discussion of what she terms the 'normative ideal of city life'. Young observes that, for many people, 'city life exerts a powerful attraction' (Young, 1990, 237). And an important part of this attraction consists in 'the pleasure and excitement of being drawn out of one's secure routine to encounter the novel, strange, and surprising' (Young, 1990, 239):

> [we] take pleasure in being open to and interested in people we experience as different. We spend a Sunday afternoon walking through Chinatown, or checking out this week's eccentric players in the park. We look for restaurants, stores and clubs with something new for us, a new ethnic food, a different atmosphere, a different crowd of people. We walk through sections of the city that we experience as having unique characters which are not ours, where people from diverse places mingle and then go home. (Young, 1990, 239)

While I think there is an important truth contained in what Young says here, I think we have to be a little careful. The vision she articulates is a strangely sanitized one. It is what Marshall Berman has called a 'pastoral' vision of modernity, 'modernity without tears' (Berman, 1983, 137). It is a vision of the modern city rich in exciting difference and diversity, yet devoid of genuine and painful moral conflict. City life as we actually experience it is a great deal more dislocated, troubled and jarring than Young's image suggests. Venturing into a new and different neighbourhood is not always the pleasurable and exciting experience Young describes; it can just as often be frightening and alienating. Part of the problem, it seems to me, is that Young focuses rather too much on 'difference' and not enough on 'conflict'.

Nevertheless, we need not infer from that reservation that modern life must therefore be a context of anomie. Such 'counter-pastoral' images as those articulated by the likes of MacIntyre and Bellah are equally flawed. Berman argues that often in fact it is precisely the uneasiness that pervades our experience of modern life that explains its attraction. The modern city, on this view, is *animated* by its contradictions (Berman, 1983, 131–71). This is a view of civic life for which 'loneliness and belonging, togetherness and estrangement live cheek by jowl; every exchanged glance, every instant of pleasure, is tinged with portents of loss' (Ignatieff, 1984, 140). This is a view of civic life like Robert Musil's Vienna, a life as made up 'of one great rhythmic beat as well as the chronic discord and mutual displacement of all its contending rhythms' (Musil, 1995, 3). What I am suggesting, then, is something that runs counter to both Bellah and Young: against the counterpastoral picture elaborated by Bellah *et al.* of lonely and alienated individuals fearfully retreating into their homogeneous enclaves *and also* against the pastoral picture elaborated by Young of beautiful, rich and untroubled diversity we may set a far more complex, ambivalent and realistic picture. Perhaps the friction and uneasiness that pervades the modern experience is part of its appeal. Many of us feel comfortable amid the life and liveliness of a modern conflicted society; this is where we feel we belong. We spend a lot of time declaiming against the impoverishment of the anonymous crowd and the modern city, yet they also hold for us a unique and irresistible appeal. This is simply inexplicable on the view that we are nothing but a collection of mutually disinterested strangers.

So, my view is that MacIntyre's claim, in the stark form in which it is put, is simply false. Pronouncements on the moral vacuity of modern life are commonplace. We are forever being reminded of the erosion of community, the advance of individualism and the estrangement it heralds. But much more remarkable, to my mind, are the multiplicity of ways in which moral life continues to flourish in modern democratic societies. We are not like the self-interested strangers MacIntyre describes. We are much more heavily implicated in the life we share with our fellow citizens. We trust each other, we make personal sacrifices for each other and we value our association. Certainly this is a rather surprising conclusion. Not only does it upset MacIntyre's assertion, but also it contradicts one of our most fundamental beliefs about community, solidarity and belonging: the belief that they all depend somehow upon substantial moral consensus, the belief that conflict is anathema to community. On the basis of that belief, MacIntyre's claim seems entirely natural. Modern democratic societies are vast and immensely complex entities marked by profound moral diversity and disagreement. The members of such societies evidently do not share in the pursuit of a common conception of the good. Our theories thus lead us to believe that we really should be nothing more than a collection of self-interested strangers. And yet we *are* more than that. It seems that our political reality contradicts our political theory and reveals a potential way in which moral community could survive, and even flourish, in conditions of conflict.

But how can this be? Given that we share neither a substantial morality, nor a strong sense of common nationality with our fellow citizens, are we not crazy to place our trust in them, to sacrifice our lifeblood (both figuratively and literally) for these people with whom we have so little in common and so much in contention? If it is true that we are not strangers to one another in MacIntyre's sense, then we need some account of why that is so. Our political theory has so far struggled to provide one. And there is another question here. If it is true that we are not strangers, then what on earth are we? We are not enemies and we are not friends (not, at least, in the conventional sense of those terms). I have suggested that there is indeed a relation between the inhabitants of modern societies, but when we try to express that relation in a theoretical vocabulary our words fail us.

These are the central problems that animate this book, which seeks to probe, and ultimately to challenge, the conventional theoretical view of the relationship between community and conflict in contemporary liberal political philosophy. The book is divided into seven chapters. In the first I seek to develop the problems I have sketched here and to explain why I believe them to be of the utmost importance to liberal political theory. There I shall argue that the task of developing an account of community capable of surviving in conditions of moral conflict can be seen to be integral to the success of the liberal enterprise. However, I shall also argue that much of our theoretical vocabulary of community, the origins of which are identifiable in the ancient philosophies of Plato and Aristotle, are wholly inadequate to the present task. For this reason, in Chapter 2 I shall seek to develop a new vocabulary for the discussion of community in contemporary liberal political philosophy, a vocabulary that draws on the insights of literature, and of fictional journey narratives in particular. I believe that the appeal to journey narratives is useful because such narratives can reveal to us different and novel ways of thinking about the shared life of a community. In this connection, I argue that the concept of a shared life should be central to theoretical discussions of community. The concept is important because it encourages a movement away from an understanding of social unity as static and towards an understanding capable of accommodating, and indeed emphasizing, temporality, flux and even conflict.

With the concept of a shared life in place, I proceed in Chapters 3, 4 and 5 to examine and assess three different models of social unity, each of which is discernible, to a greater or lesser degree, in the contemporary philosophical literature. With each of these different models, I shall associate a different form of journey narrative – pilgrimage, escape and quest. My contention is that by viewing these models of social unity as so many 'shapes' that a shared life might possess, we are able to come to a far richer understanding of the character of these models and of their adequacy as accounts of liberal community in conditions of moral conflict. I shall argue that the appropriate shape by which to conceptualize the shared life of the citizens of a modern democratic society is provided by a combination of the narratives of escape and quest. These narratives suggest a form of liberal political community which dispenses with the idea that morally meaningful association must be founded upon a shared substantial morality, or a shared comprehensive conception of the good life.

The final two chapters, 6 and 7, will seek to respond to the charge that by dispensing with the requirement of substantial moral consensus, I must necessarily evacuate my model of liberal community of any meaning and significance. Because conflict is undermining of community, the accusation runs, any model of social unity which accommodates conflict must of necessity render itself shallow and attenuated. I shall aim to respond to this charge first by suggesting, in Chapter 6, that it may be a mistake to insist that meaningful community must be founded on shared understanding. I shall argue that, very often in fact, the reverse is true: shared understandings can be the consequence of a prior, and basic, attachment which I shall characterize as a form of 'political friendship'. To this response it may be objected that by switching the emphasis from community to friendship, I have not so much solved the problem posed by conflict as shifted it. Just as community is vulnerable to erosion in the face of conflict, so too is friendship. In Chapter 7, I shall deny this by arguing that it is simply a mistake to regard conflict as a 'problem' in the first place: not only is conflict no barrier to political friendship and, hence, community; it can also in fact be construed as providing a significant source of motivation for association.

Underlying my argument is an important subsidiary concern that it would be well to register from the outset. In this introduction, I have suggested that our theoretical grasp of community appears to be contradicted by the political reality of modern democratic societies. The prevailing theoretical understanding of community and of its relationship to conflict leads us to MacIntyre's diagnosis of modern society as nothing but a collection of disinterested strangers. But I have suggested that even a cursory glance at the reality of life in a modern democratic society reveals that this diagnosis is, at best, only partially accurate. It seems to me that this is an instance of a broader tendency of political philosophy to lose contact with and, at the limit, to falsify the world of which it is concerned to make sense. It seems to me that political philosophy could benefit from a more active engagement with the political realities it seeks to address, and this book is in part intended as a small contribution to that enterprise.

Of course this observation is very far from novel. It is a worry that has been made familiar by the likes of Bernard Williams and Stuart Hampshire. In his *Innocence and Experience*, for example, Hampshire laments the 'fairy-tale quality' of so much Anglo-American moral philosophy, a philosophy from which 'the realities of politics, both contemporary and past politics, are absent' (Hampshire, 1989, 12; see also Williams, 2005). Remarks like these are often taken as a reminder of just how awful the world really is. The charge is that philosophical theories have falsified our experience by ignoring the harsh realities of life and making the world seem better and brighter than it really is, by constructing innocent utopian fairytales from which the horrors of extreme poverty, war and starvation are mysteriously absent. Certainly it is true that political philosophers have been guilty of ignoring such grim realities, but that is not all they have ignored. It is part of my concern to suggest that in some ways at least the real world is actually rather better and brighter than our philosophical 'fantasies' have suggested. Innocence comes in many guises and political theorists have been known to peddle nightmares as well as fairytales. The prospects for community in conditions of conflict are in fact rather healthier than the likes of MacIntyre would have us believe. Not all political realities have to be harsh.

1
Why Liberal Community Matters

> It is natural to conjecture that the congruence of the right and the good depends in large part upon whether a well-ordered society achieves the good of community. (John Rawls, *A Theory of Justice*, 1971, 520)

> Liberalism rejects political society as a community because, among other things, it leads to the systematic denial of basic liberties and may allow the oppressive use of the government's monopoly of (legal) force. (John Rawls, *Political Liberalism*, 1996, 146, n.13)

Liberal political philosophy has always stood in an ambivalent relation to the concept of political community. On one hand, community clearly matters a great deal to contemporary liberal political theorists. During the 1980s, the so-called communitarian critics of Rawls popularized the notion that liberalism neglects the values of community. As Michael Sandel put it, liberalism 'forgets the possibility that when politics goes well we can know a good in common that we cannot know alone' (Sandel, 1982, 183). The incredulity and hostility with which Sandel's critique was generally received confirmed that this was very far from the truth. In fact, a concern for community is evident from the very beginning of contemporary Anglo-American liberal political philosophy when, in *A Theory of Justice*, John Rawls expresses concern for the question of 'whether the contract doctrine is a satisfactory framework for understanding the values of community' (Rawls, 1999, 456). For Rawls, the well-ordered liberal society is to be conceived as a 'social union of social unions' the members of which will prize liberal institutional forms 'as good in themselves' and will experience their 'collective activity ... as a good' (Rawls, 1971, 527, 528). This concern for the achievement of community in the liberal polity has endured and has provided the subject matter of numerous books, articles and chapters. J. Donald Moon suggests that the realization of political community ought to be among the central aims of liberal political theory. Indeed, he suggests that political liberalism may be interpreted as 'a strategy to achieve political community' (Moon, 1993, 98). Chandran Kukathas insists that the dominant understanding of liberal political community is a very rich and substantive one, being that of 'a form of association in which individuals are ... deeply implicated' and which 'displays the qualities of solidarity and stability over time' (Kukathas, 2003, 189). This leads him to the rather surprising conclusion that contemporary liberals in fact 'share a great deal with their communitarian adversaries' (Kukathas, 2003, 189).

But, as told, this does seem a little odd; how could the likes of Sandel have been so seriously mistaken? If liberals are really as enthusiastic about political community as all of this suggests, how did the communitarians come to believe exactly the opposite? In truth, the liberal attitude to community is anything but straightforward. The communitarians were certainly right to think that liberals regard community with a considerable degree of caution. Community is thought potentially to be a source of great danger to liberalism because very often it seems in practice to entail a grim uniformity quite at odds with the liberal ideal. As Anthony Arblaster has written, for liberals, 'freedom is the condition which each person needs in order to fulfil himself. The thoroughgoing integration of the individual into the collective life of society must result in the cramping and distorting of the personality. But give the individual freedom and privacy: set her free from the pressures of state and society, and she will find within herself the resources to make the most of the opportunities freedom offers' (Arblaster, 1984, 43). It is this recognition of the illiberal potentiality of community that prompts Rawls's declaration that political liberalism must 'abandon the ideal of political community' (Rawls, 1996, 201).

There is evidently something of a tangle here. Liberal theorists seem unclear as to whether political community is something they should be endorsing or rejecting. This ambivalence in the liberal attitude to community reveals a fundamental tension in contemporary liberal thought and provides the focus of my inquiry. This is a book about the idea of liberal community and specifically the idea's relation to the conflicts by which modern societies are beset. Centrally, I want to explore whether it is possible to provide a model of liberal community adequate to the conditions of modernity. In this first chapter, I hope to clarify the nature of the task by explaining the source of the curious ambivalence I have identified: why do liberals seem so uncertain about community? Answering this question will require, first, consideration of why it is that liberal community matters. Why, after all, are we not content to conceive of the liberal society as a collection of mutually unconcerned strangers? Secondly, it will be necessary to inquire further into the basis of Rawls's abandonment of community. Doing so, I shall argue, reveals a rather profound difficulty for liberalism, one that renders the task of developing an adequate account of liberal community critical.

Before I begin, however, it is worth pausing just to stress what I am *not* going to try to do in the chapter. I am not going to try to explain here, or indeed anywhere else in the book, why liberal community should matter to those to whom it does not matter. My discussion is directed towards those liberals for whom community does constitute a value. I do not intend to convince those who believe otherwise that they are mistaken. In other words, then, I begin from the (not uncontroversial) presumption that liberal community does indeed matter. My concern in this chapter is to explain why it matters to those to whom it matters and also why this presents them with a rather serious problem.

Liberal political community

'Community' is a notoriously awkward term to define. Andrew Mason observes that it is a term 'used with alarming frequency' in all manner of different contexts. People talk about international community, national community, local neighbourhood community, business community, ethnic community, gay community and so on; and it is far from clear that the term is intended to denote the same sort of thing in each and every case (Mason, 2000, 1). Nevertheless, some have tried to discern a core concept of community within this morass of usages (Mason, 2000, 17–41; see also, Frazer, 1999, 47–85). While I admire these efforts, I have no intention of reconstructing them here or of attempting anything of the same order. For reasons that will, in the coming chapters, become clear, I want to avoid, as far as possible, stipulative definition of the concept. However, it is clearly important that something be said to delineate the area of concern. While I shall not attempt to provide a complete definition of community as such, I do want to provide a minimal characterization of the idea of a liberal political community in order to give us some idea of what we are talking about.

It seems natural to suppose that there is a meaningful distinction to be drawn between the idea of a society and the idea of a community. Mason suggests that a 'mere' society 'consists of people who interact with one another primarily on a contractual basis, in order to further their own self-regarding interests' (Mason, 2000, 20). In other words, a mere society may be thought to consist of the kinds of strangers we encountered in the Introduction. It seems plausible to suppose that, in the short term at least, social cohesion is possible among such strangers. Such associations may be essentially strategic and are often described in the literature as *modi vivendi*. This conception of mere society as *modus vivendi* can serve to provide us with a preliminary, negative characterization of community. Whatever else it is, a community is a non-strategic association. A community is, in some sense as yet unspecified, a *moral* association.

More specifically, the idea of a liberal political community is thought to turn on the idea of justifiability. Minimally, in other words, the liberal society will constitute a community where reasonable citizens are able morally to endorse the liberal principles of justice which structure the political institutions to which they are subject (Mason, 2000, 68–9). But the idea of justifiability central to the concept of a liberal community is developed in the literature in stronger and weaker forms. Fundamentally, a distinction is drawn between what I shall term community as *public* justifiability and community as *general* justifiability. The former of these provides the more commonplace interpretation of liberal community and is apparent in the work of John Rawls. Rawls suggests that a conception of justice achieves publicity where '(1) everyone accepts and knows that the others accept the same principles of justice, and

(2) the basic social institutions generally satisfy and are generally known to satisfy these principles' (Rawls, 1971, 5). But as Charles Larmore has written, this formulation somewhat understates Rawls's position. Publicity, for Rawls, requires rather more than that principles of justice be freely acceptable to all; publicity 'really amounts to the demand that the reasons each person has to endorse the principles be reasons the person sees others to have to endorse them as well. It requires that the principles of justice be grounded in a shared point of view' (Larmore, 2003, 371). To achieve public justifiability, and hence community, in this sense, it is necessary for principles of justice to be acceptable to each citizen for reasons that all can share.

On this view, a distinctively liberal political community is realized where citizens are able to accept, and perhaps identify themselves to some extent, with the liberal political institutions to which they are subject and recognize each other as fellow members on the rather strong grounds that their endorsement of liberal institutions is grounded in a common point of view. A subjective 'sense' of community would therefore be experienced by a person who perceived the liberal political institutions to which she was subject as morally legitimate (for reasons both she and others could endorse) and would consist in a feeling of robust enthusiasm for the common life of the polity and a keen willingness to act upon the dictates of liberal justice. Such a person would have a sense of 'belonging together' with her fellow citizens (Mason, 2000, 127).[1]

General justifiability is, by contrast, less demanding. It holds that principles of justice are adequately justifiable in so far as each citizen is able morally to endorse them. There is no requirement here that endorsement must be grounded in a shared, public point of view. This understanding of community is reflected in Mason's idea of an 'inclusive political community' (Mason, 2000, 137–42). Such a community, Mason suggests, is founded on a shared commitment to the liberal polity. 'It requires that citizens with different cultural backgrounds and conceptions of the good should be able to regard most of the polity's major institutions ... and some of its central practices as valuable on balance, and feel at home in them' (Mason, 2000, 138). However, citizens' 'reasons for thinking these institutions and practices valuable may in principle diverge considerably' (Mason, 2000, 138). Clearly it is conceivable that the conception of liberal justice upon which political institutions are based could be morally acceptable to each citizen, but for different reasons in each instance.[2]

While the ideal of public justifiability holds that community is founded on moral identification with the polity and with one's fellow citizens, general justifiability holds that an association recognizably a community requires only that citizens identify themselves morally with the polity. There is no need for citizens to have a sense of belonging *together*. In other words, there is no need for mutual identification between citizens, although Mason suggests that such identification may arise as the consequence of a shared sense of belonging to the polity (Mason, 2000, 139–40). Both interpretations of the ideal of justifiability can clearly be further developed by fleshing out the exact nature and extent of the 'identification' involved in the conceptions of liberal community they suggest.

For the moment, I shall favour a minimal definition and characterize liberal political community as follows:

> Liberal political community is, at minimum, an association of citizens who morally endorse the liberal conception of justice upon which the political institutions, to which they are subject, are founded.

This definition characterizes liberal community in terms of justifiability, but leaves open the question of whether that justifiability is general or public and also the question of precisely what 'moral endorsement' or 'identification' amounts to. The task for the advocate of liberal community on this minimal definition is therefore to explain how the liberal social order, as he or she conceives it, could constitute an object of robust enthusiasm, or more formally, to explain why the requirements of the just liberal social order would not be in tension with the reasonable beliefs of citizens about morality and the good life. If no such explanation can be provided, then the integrity of the liberal society could not be provided by the sense of community of its members and would have to be accounted for on some other basis. The obvious alternative here is advantage. If the liberal social order is not aligned to the reasonable moral commitments of those subject to it, then its cohesiveness must be explained by appeal to the strategic benefits of compliance. In such cases we characterize the liberal society not as a moral community, but as a *modus vivendi*.

Why justifiability matters

So, liberal community turns centrally on the idea of justifiability. Liberals hold that community is expressed in a shared commitment to principles of justice. If we want, therefore, to know why liberal community matters, we need to consider why justifiability matters. Why is it so important that citizens be able to identify themselves with the principles of justice and institutions to which they are subject? There are two connected answers to this question: legitimacy and stability.

Many liberals hold that it is oppressive (and, hence, illegitimate) to subject reasonable people to political institutions and strictures which are not, at least in principle, justifiable to them on terms they could reasonably accept. But this rather begs the question. Why, after all, should it matter if liberal institutions are deemed illegitimate in *this way*? Surely what really matters is that they are right and good, not that everybody accepts them. Well, not quite. As Burton Dreben explains:

> When you talk about the nature of justice, at least according to Rawls, you are not merely to come up with a theory of justice; you also have to point out why the theory that you are establishing is stable, why the society based on the theory will continue to endure indefinitely. It is not enough to come up with something that will be absolutely good in Plato's heaven; it is quite important to have something that will be good on Plato's earth and will continue to be seen as usable. (Dreben, 2003, 317)

As Rawls states, the 'aims of political philosophy depend on the society it addresses' (Rawls, 1999, 421). A theory of justice is only legitimate, on this view, if it can show why people would be motivated to act in accordance with its principles. If most people in a society are unable to identify themselves with the institutions to which they are subject, then the institutional structure will be liable to become unstable and people will not be motivated to act on the dictates of justice.[3]

Could we not simply coerce people to act upon the dictates of justice (given that we know that they are right)? Probably we could, but doing so is rather uneasy from a Rawlsian perspective.[4] From the very beginning Rawls has insisted that principles of justice must be *freely* endorsed by those subject to them. As he argues in the very early paper, 'Justice as Fairness', it is only if the 'mutual acknowledgement of principles by free persons who have no authority over one another' is possible that there can be 'true community between persons in their common practices; otherwise their relations will appear to them as founded to some extent on force' (Rawls, 1999, 59). Because liberty matters, it is important to show, by non-coercive means, that it would be unreasonable for a person to regard the dictates of justice as an infringement of her freedom.

So, it is essentially for stability's sake that liberals value community. If citizens are able morally to identify themselves with the institutions to which they are subject, then they will be far more inclined to act in accordance with the requirements of those institutions thereby improving the stability of the order. The citizen who conceives of himself as integrated in the liberal political community will, as Ronald Dworkin suggests, 'count his own life as diminished – a less good life than he might have had – if he lives in an unjust community, no matter how hard he has tried to make it just' (Dworkin, 2000, 233). Of course, as Dworkin stresses, the achievement of community in this sense will not *guarantee* justice and stability, injustice 'is the upshot of too many other factors', but it should certainly help (Dworkin, 2000, 233). Brian Barry seems to concur:

> Liberal democracies are very unlikely to produce just outcomes unless their citizens have certain attitudes towards one another. It must be accepted on all hands that the interests of everyone must count equally, and that there are no groups whose members' views are to be automatically discounted. Equally important is a willingness on the part of citizens to make sacrifices for the common good ... Moreover, citizens do not just as a matter of fact have to be willing to make sacrifices; it is also necessary that citizens should have firm expectations of one another to the effect that they will be prepared to give up money, leisure and perhaps even life itself if the occasion arises. (Barry, 2001, 80)

The general thought is simply that the liberal political order is likely to work better and last longer where citizens identify themselves with the principles of justice that structure the order. That is why justifiability, and hence community, is important to liberals.

But it is not clear that just any kind of justifiability (any kind of community) will do here. There is a real question of whether shared identification with the principles of justice is really enough to deliver the kinds of communal attitudes necessary to secure the stability of a just, liberal political order. Numerous communitarian and nationalist thinkers have argued that it is not. For example, David Miller writes:

> The kind of ties we are looking for are not external and mechanical, but involve each person seeing his life as part and parcel of the wider group, so that the question of how well his own life is going depends in some measure on how well the community as a whole is faring. This brings in issues of common good, historical identity, and so forth which reach far beyond the scope of distributive justice. Rawls's notion that adherence to a shared conception of distributive justice could form a sufficient basis for community is quite implausible (Miller, 1989, 60).

On this account, mere agreement on principles of justice is, as Yael Tamir suggests, 'too thin, and is insufficient to ensure the continued existence of a closed community in which members care for each other's welfare, as well as for the well-being of future generations' (Tamir, 1993, 118). What is needed, presumably, is what Dworkin calls 'integration'. Integration is achieved when citizens 'recognize that the community has a communal life, and that the success or failure of their own lives is ethically dependent on the success or failure of that communal life' (Dworkin, 2000, 231). When citizens are integrated in this way, we may suppose that they would normally be motivated to care for each other's welfare in the required ways. But it is far from clear that agreement on principles of justice alone could plausibly be thought to provide an adequate basis for this intensity of concern.

So, not just any kind of justifiability will suffice. The kind of stability that egalitarian liberals seek will not be delivered by general justifiability and the shallow 'inclusive political community' defended by Mason. It is not clear that a sense of belonging to the polity alone is sufficient to promote the kinds of attitudes *between citizens* necessary to sustain a stable liberal order, certainly not one that requires significant redistribution of resources. Liberal principles must be publicly justifiable in the strong sense that they must be viewed as expressing the shared point of view of citizens. Citizens must feel that they belong not only to the polity, but also together.

But where, then, is this sense of belonging together supposed to come from? How is 'integration' and the sense that one's life is 'part and parcel of the wider group' to be achieved? Mason suggests that a sense of belonging together may be provided by the belief among citizens 'that they shared a history, religion, ethnicity, mother tongue, culture or conception of the good' (Mason, 2000, 127). The nationalists suggest that what is needed is, unsurprisingly, an ethically substantive, solidaristic national identity. As Miller suggests, Rawls's redistributive scheme is 'hard to justify unless the parties in question share a common nationality' (Miller, 1995, 93; see also Tamir, 1993). Will Kymlicka expresses some uneasiness about the idea of a shared national identity in a multination state, but nevertheless feels that some kind of shared identity, focused perhaps on national symbols, is required for social unity. As he remarks, if 'we look to strongly patriotic but culturally diverse countries like the United States or Switzerland, the basis for a shared identity often seems to be pride in certain historical achievements (e.g. the founding of the American Republic). This shared pride is one of the bases of the strong sense of American political identity, constantly reinforced in their citizenship literature and school curriculum' (Kymlicka, 1996, 189). The central point is that all of these authors think that a sense of belonging together will only arise from some form of *deep commonality* among citizens, a 'deep reason why they should associate together' (Mason, 2000, 127). And all, bar Mason, believe that such a sense of belonging together is a prerequisite for social justice.

My concern here has been to explain why it might be that community matters to those liberals for whom it matters. We now have a possible answer to that question. Community matters because it is often thought that a workable and stable liberal egalitarian order strongly implies that the citizens subject to it will have a sense of belonging together. It is important, then, for liberals to provide a plausible account of community because their theories of social justice will be damagingly incomplete (even illegitimate) if they do not.

Community and pluralism

But, if all of this is right, why are liberals so uneasy about the idea of community? If a sense of communal belonging together is widely thought to be necessary to secure the stability of the liberal polity, why does Rawls later call for its rejection? Rawls insists that community must be abandoned because a genuinely free society will necessarily be a society characterized by a plurality of moral, religious and philosophical doctrines and will consequently be unable to achieve community (understood as deep commonality) without compromising its commitment to freedom.

Pluralism is the natural consequence of 'the activities of human reason under enduring free institutions' (Rawls, 1996, xxvi). If we leave people to their own devices, free, within certain limits, to think and do as they please, they will inevitably arrive at different, and possibly conflicting, beliefs about morality and the good life. Consequently, any genuinely liberal society will be a site of moral disagreement. This is the 'fact of pluralism':

> The diversity of reasonable comprehensive religious, philosoph-
> ical, and moral doctrines found in modern democratic societies is
> not a mere historical condition that may soon pass away; it is a
> permanent feature of the public culture of democracy. Under the
> political and social conditions secured by the basic rights and
> liberties of free institutions, a diversity of conflicting and irrecon-
> cilable ... comprehensive doctrines will come about and persist if
> such diversity does not already obtain. (Rawls, 1996, 36)

Moreover, it is not open to us, as liberals, to regard the permanence of pluralism as an unfortunate condition. Reasonable people reasoning under conditions of freedom can be expected, Rawls suggests, to arrive at different and conflicting beliefs about morality and the good life. 'Different conceptions of the world can reasonably be elaborated from different standpoints and diversity arises in part from our distinct perspectives. It is unrealistic ... to suppose that all our differences are rooted solely in ignorance and perversity, or else in the rivalries for power, status, or economic gain' (Rawls, 1996, 58). Not only is pluralism an inevitable feature of liberal societies, it is also in some cases a reasonable feature. So reasonable pluralism, too, is a fact, and to see it as a disaster would be 'to see the exercise of reason under conditions of freedom itself as a disaster' (Rawls, 1996, xxvi–xxvii). If we are committed to free institutions, then we must acknowledge the reasonableness of their inevitable by-products of which conflict about morality and the good life is one.

But now the fact of reasonable and permanent pluralism seems to present a real problem for the advocate of liberal community. If a liberal society is a society necessarily marked by reasonable plural-ism, then it seems that its citizens will necessarily lack any *deep* reason for associating together. And it is important to emphasize here that, for Rawls at least, this is a structural inevitability of the free society. If the deep commonality that community requires involves a shared conception of the good life, then the members of a genuinely free society will necessarily lack a sense of community. For Rawls, a continuing shared conception of the good among liberal citizens 'can be maintained only by the oppressive use of state power' (Rawls, 1996, 37), and, quite clearly, such oppression is simply unacceptable from a liberal point of view. This is why political liberalism abandons the ideal of community: it is – or appears to be – at odds with the fundamental liberal commitment to free institutions.

But all of this places the Rawlsian liberal in a rather awkward posi-tion. On one hand, it is felt by many that community is essential to the stability of a just liberal order, yet on the other hand it is also widely supposed that a just liberal order necessarily *precludes* the achievement of community. The dark fear, then, is that liberalism is a self-defeating doctrine. It denies the possibility of justly achieving the very thing it needs (community) in order to sustain itself. The only way of overcoming this problem within the limits of the liberal argument would be to show that a liberal political community, whose members have a sense of belonging together, could emerge in conditions of pronounced moral diversity and conflict. However, and as I noted at the very beginning of the book, many people do not really believe that community can emerge in conditions of pro-nounced moral diversity and conflict. In fact, the suspicion is that conflict is positively destructive of community. It is thought that the idea of the liberal society 'as a social union which enables indi-viduals to know a good in common that they cannot know alone, expresses a wish for a degree of social unity which is simply inconsistent with the extent of diversity, mobility, and disagreement in the modern world' (Kukathas, 2003, 258). Any desire we may have for genuine community must go unfulfilled, for community is vitiated by conflict; and conflict is eternal.

So, now we can see why it is often regarded as both vital and extremely difficult to provide a plausible account of liberal community. It is vital because without such an account, the liberal political order may not work properly. It is extremely difficult because liberalism is morally committed to resisting the conditions in which community is thought most likely to flourish. The liberal for whom community matters is thus left with the task of explaining how a sense of belonging together could be achieved among people who have very little in common with one another. This can seem a rather quixotic enterprise, because it is traditionally assumed that a sense of belonging together necessarily presupposes some form of commonality. I want now to turn to this traditional assumption and to examine it in some detail. Why do we think that conflict is undermining of community?

Community and consensus

The idea that conflict is undermining of community is one with ancient origins. It is given its most striking and influential articulation in Plato's *Republic*. Plato urges us to conceive of the good community as analogous to the tripartite soul of a good individual. Just as the individual's soul is divided into higher (reasoning) and lower (passionate and desiring) parts, so too is the community divided into the higher (governors) and the lower (governed). Furthermore, just as an individual soul in good order is marked by a harmony between these parts, so too is a community in good order. As Plato explains of the good man, harmony is essential:

> Once he is his own ruler, and is well-regulated, and has internal concord; once he has treated the three factors as if they were literally the three defining notes of an octave – low, high, and middle – and has created a harmony out of them and however many notes there may be in between; once he has bound all the factors together and made himself a perfect unity instead of a plurality, self-disciplined and internally attuned: then and only

then does he act – if he acts – to acquire property or look after his body or play a role in government or do some private business. In the course of this activity, it is conduct which preserves and promotes this inner condition of his that he regards as moral and describes as fine. (Plato, 1993, 443d–e)

Analogously, the good community is marked by 'a harmony between the naturally worse and naturally better elements of society as to which of them should rule both in a community and in every individual' (Plato, 1993, 432a–b). Conversely, of course, the immoral individual is an individual internally ruptured and divided against himself: an individual in conflict. Such internal conflict 'constitutes not only immorality, but also indiscipline, cowardice, and stupidity – in a word, badness of any kind' (Plato, 1993, 444b). Likewise, a bad community is one tainted by conflict.

In fact, Plato goes a bit further than this to indicate that associations divided by conflict do not in fact deserve the name of 'community' at all:

They should have a more capacious title, ... since each of them is not so much a community as a great many communities. ... Minimally, they contain two warring communities – one consisting of the rich and one of the poor. Then each of these two contains quite a number of further communities. It would be quite wrong to treat this plurality as a unity. (Plato, 1993, 422e–423a)[5]

Consequently, Plato seeks to expunge all potential sources of value conflict, such as private property and exclusive sexual relationships, from his vision of community. On this view, it seems that complete consensus (or near complete consensus) is a necessary condition of community. The degree to which conflict is present in any given association is the degree to which that association has ceased to be a community.

Aristotle is very critical of Plato's account of community and it may thus be tempting to think that he represents a departure from the Platonist identification of community and consensus. Aristotle argues that, by seeking to eliminate all sources of conflict, Plato actually weakens the association, for 'the unity which he commends would be like that of the lovers in the *Symposium*, who, as Aristophanes says, desire to grow together in the excess of their affection, and from being two to become one, in which case one or both would certainly perish' (Aristotle, 1984, 1262b10–15). The problem with this kind of unity is that no relationships involving such a high order of intensity and intimacy can possibly be achieved at the level of the political community. By trying to force citizens to view one another as fellow family members, we inevitably dilute the meaning of 'family' (Aristotle, 1984, 1262b15–20). Moreover, it is not altogether clear that Aristotle thinks that we should even *want* the kind of unity that Plato envisages, were it attainable. As Martha Nussbaum remarks, 'Aristotle argues at length that this sort of [Platonist] conflict-free unity is not the sort of unity appropriate to the *polis*, since it destroys personal separateness, an essential ingredient of human goodness' (Nussbaum, 2001, 353).⁶

But note that this does not in fact entail any significant departure from the fundamental idea of community as consensus. To be sure, Aristotle does not support the kind of unity envisaged by Plato, but there is no doubt that Aristotle does believe that agreement provides the basis of community. As he suggests in the *Nicomachean Ethics*, 'friendship ... seems to be the bond that holds communities together, and lawgivers seem to attach more importance to it than to justice; because concord seems to be something like friendship, and concord is their primary object – that and eliminating faction, which is enmity' (Aristotle, 1976, 1155a20–30). Just as was the case in Plato's account, we find here the notion that to the extent that an association is divided by conflict, the community is threatened: 'every cause of difference makes a breach in a city' (Aristotle, 1984, 1303b10–15). Once again, then, community is consensus; and the greater the consensus, the more united the community will be. Where Aristotle differs from Plato is in his view of the role of conflict in the good life. Plato takes the view that, since conflict poses a threat to community, it is necessary (or advisable) to elim-inate all potential grounds of conflict. The good life is one of total harmony. Aristotle does not disagree that conflict poses a threat to community, but insists that the peculiar good of community is partly constituted by its *vulnerability*. The fragility of the unity we achieve is a vital constituent of the good of that unity.⁷ That is to say, it is the *possibility* of conflict, and not conflict itself, which is vital to the community. Aristotle's quarrel with Plato turns not on his (Plato's) concern to eliminate faction, but rather on his concern to eliminate the *possibility* of faction.

The identification of community with consensus made familiar by Plato and Aristotle has proven extremely influential. It permeates most contemporary political thought and underpins the conviction that the only way of accounting for the value of community is through the detection of what I have termed 'deep commonality'. We believe that community stands in an antagonistic relation to conflict: the more pronounced the conflicts they accommodate, the more shallow and attenuated our communities must become. As Kukathas puts it: 'the greater the diversity of cultural groups with independent moral traditions within a polity, the less the extent of social unity within that political society' (Kukathas, 2003, 166). Accordingly, social unity and diversity can be combined only 'if that unity is a shallow unity' (Kukathas, 2003, 189). In other words, liberal political community might be achieved, but only if we are prepared to 'water down our expectations of social unity' (Kukathas, 2003, 189). That is all very well, and we might regard Mason's account of inclusive political community as one such 'watered-down' account; but, as I have suggested, it is not in fact clear that accounts of community so attenuated will actually be thick enough to promote the kinds of attitudes and the degree of integration required in order to secure the stability of the liberal political order. If Kukathas is right about the relationship between community and conflict, then it seems that the just and stable society may be an impossible dream.

Community in practice

But there is something really rather odd in this deeply ingrained understanding of the relation between community and conflict as antagonistic: it seems to be contradicted by the experience of modern societies. Modern democratic societies are contexts of pronounced moral diversity and disagreement; it is far from clear that we have anything 'deep' in common with our fellow citizens. The prevailing theoretical understanding of the relationship between community and conflict would thus encourage us to think that these societies will be contexts of estrangement. In so far as the members of modern societies do not share a moral outlook or a substantive national identity, our theories lead us to suspect that their cohesion can only plausibly be explained in strategic terms. But, as I argued in the Introduction, this just does not seem to be the case. Many of the members of modern democratic societies seem in fact to conceive of themselves as integrated in the common life of the society: they trust one another and they display concern for one another. And, importantly, these practices of mutuality seem to operate with little or no regard for the facts of moral diversity. We do not generally find it necessary to check the moral values or national identity of the stranger in the street before we are willing to trust his report of the time according to his wristwatch. We donate our blood anonymously; it is not open to us to specify an acceptable range of moral beliefs which must be held by any prospective recipient as a condition of meriting our concern. And normally people do not want to make such a specification.

In other words, I am suggesting that there is a tension between our theories of social unity, which we have inherited from the ancient Greeks, and the practice of social unity in modern democratic societies. One response to this would be to resolve the tension in favour of theory. We could simply conclude that we moderns are foolish to participate in these practices of mutuality with our fellow citizens, for they are groundless. But for the advocate of liberal political community it is surely rather tempting to explore the alternative: what if our theories are wrong and it is possible for a morally significant political relationship to flourish in conditions of conflict? If such a relationship can exist in practice, then perhaps it could serve to resolve the theoretical problem I have identified. Perhaps it could help us to explain how the ideal interpretation of a liberal community as a publicly justifiable political association marked by a significant degree of mutuality could be realized in conditions of reasonable pluralism.

In my view, there is very little in our actual experience of contemporary political life to confirm the belief that mutuality depends for its existence on the sharing of values or, for that matter, identities. Increasingly it seems that the Platonist association of community and consensus constitutes a serious distraction for the contemporary liberal political theorist; it prevents us from recognizing that there are genuine possibilities for mutuality in contexts of pluralism and conflict. If we look at the political reality before us we shall see that community and conflict often go hand-in-hand. This is my hypo-thesis: the Platonist image of conflict as anathema to community is a myth which is unsupported by experience. It is deeply unclear why we should continue to believe, against the facts of our experi-ence, that community is consensus. Indeed, the maintenance of this belief can now begin to seem rather damaging. The insistence that community is unrealizable (or only imperfectly realizable) in condi-tions of pluralism blinds us to the real prospects of the idea of liberal community in the modern context. This is a concern raised by Ignatieff when he asks whether there can be 'a language of belonging adequate to Los Angeles'. Put like that, he suggests, 'the answer can only seem to be no,' but that is just because our 'polit-ical images of civic belonging remain haunted by the classical polis, by Athens, Rome and Florence' (Ignatieff, 1984, 139–140). The Platonist fairytale that community is consensus has infected our language and fundamentally obscured the character and prospects of liberal solidarity.

It thus seems that a solution to the theoretical puzzle confronting the advocate of liberal community might, so to speak, be right under our noses in the everyday public life of a modern liberal democracy. However, making use of this solution is going to be harder than one might suppose. The problem is that the solution is theoretically 'mute'. Modern societies, reveal a moral bond capable of flourishing in conditions of conflict and yet we have no theoret-ical language with which to express that bond. As I have suggested, our theoretical language insists that any such bond is impossible. As Ignatieff remarks, words 'like fraternity, belonging and community are so soaked with nostalgia and utopianism that they are nearly useless as guides to the real possibilities of solidarity in modern society. Modern life has changed the possibilities of civic solidarity, and our language stumbles behind like an overburdened porter with a mountain of old cases' (Ignatieff, 1984, 138). If we are to have a chance of resolving the apparent tension between the liberal com-mitments to community and conflict, we must first 'find a language for our need for belonging which is not just a way of expressing nostalgia, fear and estrangement from modernity' (Ignatieff, 1984, 139). And this is not only a matter of theoretical urgency; Ignatieff voices the practical concern that if we are unable to find a language of community appropriate to our times, then we will be liable to fall back on the 'easy laments about the alienation of modern life' which have become such a pervasive feature of our culture and we will lose the very real bond we share (Ignatieff, 1984, 141). 'Without a language adequate to this moment we risk losing ourselves in resignation towards the portion of life that has been allotted to us. Without the light of language, we risk becoming strangers to our better selves' (Ignatieff, 1984, 142).

Summary

In this chapter I have sought to make sense of the ambivalent relationship between liberalism and community. On one hand, I have suggested that many liberals recognize that mutuality and community provide a vital constituent of the stability of a just society. However, they are also well aware that liberal societies must be sites of moral conflict. Consequently, and on the belief that such conflict presents a barrier to the realization of community, they have been encouraged to temper their expectations of social unity.

However, I have suggested that this last might be a mistake. The actual experience of modern liberal democracies casts the belief that conflict is a barrier to moral association into doubt. Real life suggests that mutuality is entirely possible between moral strangers, and even perhaps moral adversaries, and thus revives our hopes for the possibility of a substantive liberal community. The aim of this book is to develop a theoretical account of liberal solidarity compatible with the pronounced moral conflict that constitutes a permanent feature of free societies. However, there is a real question here of how one is now supposed to proceed. If our current theoretical vocabulary of community is so 'soaked with nostalgia and utopianism' as to be 'nearly useless' as a guide to liberal solidarity, then what are we supposed to do? How can we free ourselves from this inarticulacy? Ignatieff argues that we must turn to art and literature, for it is 'the painters and the writers, not the politicians or the social scientists, who have been able to find a language for the joy of modern life, its fleeting and transient solidarity' (Ignatieff, 1984, 141). I propose to take this suggestion seriously. In the next chapter, I shall elaborate and defend a new vocabulary for the discussion of community, one that draws on the insights of literature.

2
The Shape of a Shared Life

> Words like fraternity, belonging and community are so
> soaked with nostalgia and utopianism that they are nearly
> useless as guides to the real possibilities of solidarity in
> modern society. Modern life has changed the possibilities
> of civic solidarity, and our language stumbles behind like
> an overburdened porter with a mountain of old cases.
> (Ignatieff, 1984, 138)

In the previous chapter, I set the central challenge of this book: to
show how a substantive sense of liberal political community might
coexist with the pronounced moral diversity of a modern democratic society. In this connection, I questioned the deeply ingrained
assumption that disagreement constitutes a barrier to community.
With Michael Ignatieff, I suggested that our language of community
and belonging might actually blind us to the 'real possibilities of
solidarity in modern society'. But this claim leaves in its wake a
residual problem: how are we now to proceed? How can we articulate an account of liberal community when our vocabulary is 'nearly
useless'? Ignatieff advises a turn to literature. There we might find 'a
language for the joy of modern life, its fleeting and transient solidarity' (Ignatieff, 1984, 141). In this chapter I want to pursue this suggestion. I want to develop a new vocabulary for the discussion of
political community which draws on the insights of literature. In so
doing, I shall elaborate and defend the method I intend to deploy in
the following three chapters in which I shall seek to articulate three
distinct accounts of liberal community the outlines of which are

informed by the outlines of three different kinds of fictional journey narrative.

The idea of a shared life

In the previous chapter I suggested that our ordinary language of community distorts our perception of the possibilities for solidarity. The ordinary usage of the term 'community' is closed and inflexible; it is ideologically burdened with questionable assumptions, all too often contradicted by the experience of modernity. It is thus vital that we find some way of developing a degree of critical distance from the term. I hope to achieve this by substituting (or at least supplementing) the idea of 'community' with the idea of a 'shared life'. I think we should move away from the idea of social associations as static, monolithic analytical entities and towards a conception of association as dynamic, and as possessing temporal depth.

We find it important to render our social world coherent and intelligible. We may not know many of our fellow citizens, yet as I suggested in the Introduction we find the notion that this makes us simply strangers to one another inaccurate. There is a sense, particularly in the modern context, in which community and solidarity are *invisible*. Benedict Anderson points out that 'the members of even the smallest nation will never know most of their fellow-members, meet them, or even hear of them' (Anderson, 1991, 6). Similarly, and as I have already noted, Ignatieff writes of the 'silent relation' between the inhabitants of a modern welfare state (Ignatieff, 1984, 10). At any given time it is liable, on the surface at least, to be profoundly unclear as to why and how we are specially bound to those around us, or indeed whether we are bound to them at all. And this is a real problem. The 'silence' of modern political relationships, the fact that they are mediated by the state, 'walls us off from each other. We are responsible for each other, but we are not responsible to each other' (Ignatieff, 1984, 10). The danger here is that we achieve a moral relation of equality only at the cost of a genuine sense of community and solidarity. If we can find no way of bringing these silent moral relations to life, then we shall 'remain a society of strangers' (Ignatieff, 1984, 18).

It is for this reason that Anderson introduces the idea of 'imagined community'. The connections between the members of an association may be invisible or silent, 'yet in the minds of each lives the image of their communion' (Anderson, 1991, 6). Andrew Mason helpfully expands on Anderson's idea:

> By an 'imagin*ed* community' Anderson does not mean an imaginary community. Imagined communities are real enough, but their existence depends upon people conceiving of themselves as related to one another. People who have never met can do this by subsuming their relationship to each other under some description, for example, compatriot, fellow Sikh. Mutual recognition of this kind can be secured in various ways (for example by dress, attendance at ceremonies, participation in rituals) and does not require personal acquaintance. (Mason, 2000, 40)

Anderson's imagined community also informs Charles Taylor's idea of a 'social imaginary', which describes 'the ways people imagine their social existence, how they fit together with others, how things go on between them and their fellows, the expectations that are normally met, and the deeper normative notions and images that underlie these expectations' (Taylor, 2004, 23). On this view, community resides in the way in which we describe and conceptualize our shared existence.

We might think of the process of working out exactly how we fit together with our fellow citizens as a process of social 'map-making'. David Kahane writes that we make sense of our daily interactions with unknown others 'by placing individuals on a map of social constellations that also describes [our] own sense of belonging' (Kahane, 1999, 280):

> Especially when it comes to casual interactions with strangers and acquaintances, your affective stance toward these others – be it open or suspicious, benevolent or hostile – is constituted in large part by this sort of social map-making. To the extent that you positively appreciate these others – experience a bond with them in spite of all you do not know – this derives from a sense of shared and divergent memberships. (Kahane, 1999, 281)

And it is important to emphasize here that comprehending membership has a temporal dimension. Our social interactions with unknown others are 'mediated by stories' which naturally extend forwards and backwards through time (Kahane, 1999, 280). I do not just understand my relation to my fellow citizen as a 'snapshot' moment. Rather, my understanding incorporates considerations concerning the way in which we were related yesterday, and the way in which I expect us to be related tomorrow. The way in which we imagine community in our daily lives is typically not as an abstract and static theoretical construct, but as an ongoing, and relatively concrete, narrative (Taylor, 2004, 23). Our sense of com-munity (or the lack thereof) very often resides in the stories we tell ourselves about our shared lives.

So, for example, I hope to understand myself by telling a story that makes something like a unity of my life. This story will make reference to others, especially close friends and relatives, who have impinged significantly on my life. When I encounter a stranger in the course of my day, the man who sells me a cup of coffee, I rarely rest content with the idea that he is simply alien on the grounds that he does not fit into my story as it currently stands; instead, I tell a larger story, a story big enough to accommodate both of us. Equally, when I think about my fellow citizens, I am able to make a community of us (if I am able) by telling a story broad enough to include us all.

Because stories are central to our practical comprehension of the communities to which we take ourselves to belong, I think it impor-tant that we accord to narrative a more prominent place in our the-ories of community and association. At first sight, this might seem rather impracticable: the stories we tell to make sense of our shared lives will be massively complex and will vary dramatically from case to case. Certainly, I do not mean to suggest that we should consider in any particular depth the specific stories that people tell; that would be impractical. But I think we can draw an important and fruitful distinction here between form and content. While the stories people tell to make sense of their shared lives will be highly various, I suspect that those stories will be organized and patterned in accordance with a range of different genres or shapes. At this stage, that is simply a speculation, but it does not strike me as absurd. Western literature has provided us with a vast range of dif-ferent stories, and a much more limited set of shapes. We could not, that is to say, expect to engage with every journey story that has ever been told, but we can engage more abstractly with the broader *categories* of journey stories: journeys of pilgrimage, escape and quest. The political theorist can acknowledge and accommodate the important role of story-telling in the social construction of community by reflecting on the variety of different shapes that a shared life can possess.

Because political community is in large part practically constituted by (and reflected in) the stories we tell about our shared lives, I contend that an adequate understanding of political community requires an adequate understanding of the shape of a shared life. It is with this idea, and not with the ideologically overburdened and rather utopian concept of community, that the study of liberal political association should begin. I recommend this move essentially because it seems that when, in practice, we tell stories of how our lives are shared with others, we do not necessarily invoke the kinds of assumptions, relating to consensus and fixity, that have somehow found their way into the conception of community that has come to dominate the theoretical literature. The idea of a shared life thus allows us to gain some kind of critical leverage on the prevailing understanding of community and to discern a more extensive range of communal possibilities.

In order to understand how our shared lives could plausibly be narrated, we need to look at the ways in which shared lives have been narrated across our history. It is at this point that the study of literature becomes indispensable to political philosophy. As D.Z. Phillips suggests, literature can serve as a powerful 'source of reminders (not examples) from which philosophy can benefit in wrestling with issues concerning the firm or slackening hold of various perspectives in human life' (Phillips, 1982, 1). My contention is that literary narratives in general, and fictional journey narratives in particular, can help to remind us of the variety of ways in which it is both possible and common to understand and live a shared life.

Now, it seems to me that within this general claim are three particularly controversial specific claims each of which requires considerable elaboration and defence. These are the controversial claims:

1. Something is lost where we do not conceive of communities as shared *narratives* extending through time.

2. Consideration of *journey* narratives can help us to appreciate and assess the variety of forms that the shared life of a community might take.

3. The most relevant kinds of journey narratives for us to consider are *fictional* journey narratives.

Each of the following three sections is devoted to the consideration of one of these claims.

Narratives

Of almost any life, individual or shared, it is possible to tell a story. All but the most chaotic of lives may be characterized in narrative form. That is to say, almost all lives may be attributed 'a certain sort of *developmental* and hence temporal *unity* or *coherence*' (Strawson, 2004, 439). Furthermore, the activity of narrating individual lives is very widespread. We tell stories about our own lives and about the lives of others. These activities are so common that we have given them specific names: autobiography and biography. For better or for worse, libraries and bookshops are filled with the fruits of these activities. Furthermore, and as I have already indicated, we also narrate shared lives. We attribute developmental coherence to conti-nents, nations, cities, families. Again, this activity is very wide-spread. Any given community can be thought of as possessing a story or set of stories. For example, we might think of the story of an immigrant cultural community in the liberal society. Perhaps the community's story begins as an escape from an oppressive political regime, or economic destitution abroad and then merges first into a story of home-founding in a new and unfamiliar context and finally into a story of quest for some kind of equal political recognition in the eyes of the state. It is through such stories that most of us make sense of the communities in which we take ourselves to move.

This much, I think, is relatively uncontroversial. All I have claimed so far is that it is both possible and commonplace in the modern context to imagine community in the form of a narrative. I have made neither of two related claims which I take to be a great deal more contentious: that, naturally, people *always* narrate their communal lives and that people *should* narrate their communal lives. In his article, 'Against Narrativity', Galen Strawson challenges precisely this sort of argument. Strawson distinguishes between two different modes of self-experience: the 'Episodic' mode and the 'Narrative' mode. He describes his own self-experience as Episodic:

> I have a past, like any human being, and I know perfectly well that I have a past. I have a respectable amount of factual knowledge about it, and I also remember some of my past experiences 'from the inside', as philosophers say. And yet I have absolutely no sense of my life as a narrative with form, or indeed as a narrative without form. Absolutely none. Nor do I have any great or special interest in my past. Nor do I have a great deal of concern for my future. (Strawson, 2004, 433)

This is what it is to be Episodic; Strawson characterizes it as a 'happy-go-lucky' attitude, an attitude that makes no effort to construct a narrative unity of one's life. Such activity strikes the Episodic agent as entirely unnecessary and indeed quite alien. Strawson's central thesis is that there are a great many Episodic people and that there is nothing regrettable in that. He insists that it is 'just not true that there is only one good way for human beings to experience their being in time. There are deeply non-Narrative people and there are good ways to live that are deeply non-Narrative' (Strawson, 2004, 429).

I have no desire to question the claim that there are non-Narrative people. My suspicion is that non-Narrativity is far less widespread than Strawson seems to think, but nothing hangs on that for my present argument. What I do want to claim is that a full appreciation of community requires the kind of narrative understanding I have indicated. I shall claim, with Alasdair MacIntyre, that 'there is no way to give us an understanding of any society, including our own, except through the stock of stories which constitute its initial dramatic resources' (MacIntyre, 1985, 216). In the absence of such an understanding, we will necessarily miss much of the character, significance and value of the attachments comprising the different forms of communal life available to us. This does not directly contravene Strawson's claim that there are good ways for individuals to live that are deeply non-Narrative, but it does entail that communal attachments could play only an extremely shallow role in a non-Narrative life, and this I take to be something that Strawson would want to deny.

In fact, I shall seek to defend this claim by first asserting something that Strawson explicitly denies: that Episodics 'cannot really know true friendship' (Strawson, 2004, 449). Why should we imagine that narrativity is a necessary condition of 'true friendship'? We should do so, in my view, because the idea and knowledge of a *common history* is central to the value of friendship. This is an idea made familiar by Aristotle whose account of friendship regularly stresses the significance of its temporal extension. Consider, for example, his observation that perfect, virtue friends 'need time and intimacy; for as the saying goes, you cannot get to know each other until you have eaten the proverbial quantity of salt together. Nor can one man accept another, or the two become friends, until each has proved to the other that he is worthy of love, and so won his trust. ... The wish for friendship develops rapidly, but friendship does not' (Aristotle, 1976, 1156b23–1157a). I think the importance of temporal extension to friendship reveals the inadequacy of Strawson's claim that there are good ways for individuals to live that are non-narrative, because it suggests that non-narrative people cannot really have any friends. Most of us would be inclined to think that any life without real friends is of necessity going to be a rather impoverished life.

To see this, consider first a slightly bizarre thought experiment suggested by Mark Bernstein:

> I have a wife, Nancy, whom I love very much. Let us suppose that I were informed that tomorrow, my wife Nancy would no longer be part of my life, that she would leave and forever be unseen and unheard of by me. But, in her stead, a Nancy* would appear, a qualitatively indistinguishable individual from Nancy. Nancy and Nancy* would look precisely alike, act precisely alike, think precisely alike, indeed would be alike in all physical and mental details. (Bernstein, 1985, 287)

Clearly, we can generalize this example to the case of friendship. Suppose that you are informed that tomorrow, your best friend is to be removed and replaced by best friend*. Best friend* is absolutely identical to your best friend in every way. Bernstein's response to his thought experiment is that he would be very upset by this turn of events, but this he finds puzzling: 'since we can hypothesize that

Nancy* who loved Mark* knew nothing of this exchange program, it appears as if she would love me – just as much and in identical fashion to Nancy's loving me. So why do I care, why am I so upset at the prospect' (Bernstein, 1985, 288)? It seems to me that there is nothing particularly mysterious about one's feeling upset by the prospect of having one's wife removed from one's life, never to be seen again. The more troubling issue raised by Bernstein's thought experiment concerns why we would not be inclined to care for the doppelganger as much as we do for the original. Presuming that we would not, why would we not feel the same way about our best friend* as we do about our best friend? Is it rational for us to feel differently about the replacement?

A slightly less far-fetched example is provided by Antoine de Saint-Exupery's *The Little Prince*, as discussed by Joseph Raz in his *Value, Respect and Attachment*. Saint-Exupery's novel tells the story of a little prince who loves a rose. One day, however, the little prince makes a shocking discovery. He comes upon a garden full of roses, all of which are identical to his rose. This is what the little prince says to himself:

> 'I thought that I was rich, with a flower that was unique in all the world; and all I had was a common rose ... That does not make me a very great prince.' And he lay down ... and cried. (Saint-Exupery, 2002, 60–2)

This is a similar problem told from a different direction. Suppose that you discovered that the world was full of thousands of people all of whom were exactly the same (or at least very much the same) as your best friend. Like the little prince, we want to say that there is something *special* about our best friend, something that distinguishes her from all the other best friend*s. But what could it possibly be?

Later in the story, the little prince finds the answer:

> [To all the other roses he says this,] 'You are not at all like my rose ... As yet you are nothing. ... You are beautiful, but you are empty ... One could not die for you. To be sure, an ordinary passer-by would think that my rose looked just like you ... But in herself alone she is more important than all the hundreds of you

other roses: because it is she that I have watered; because it is she that I have put under the glass globe; because it is she that I have sheltered behind the screen; because it is for her that I have killed the caterpillars ... because it is she that I have listened to when she grumbled, or boasted, or even sometimes when she said nothing. Because she is *my* rose.' (Saint-Exupery, 2002, 68)

As Raz suggests, the little prince's rose 'is not perceptually unique, but unique she is, made unique by the history of their love' (Raz, 2001, 22). The little prince's rose is special to him because *he grew her*. They have shared a common history and it is through an appreciation of that history that the little prince comprehends the distinctiveness of his attachment. In order to explain why it is rational for you to be unmoved by best friend*, therefore, it is necessary to appeal to the facts of a unique shared history. You have shared nothing with your best friend*, and everything with your best friend.

So, this is my claim: in order fully to comprehend the value of our friendships, we need to take into account the facts of our shared life. Deprived of that narrative understanding of the relationship, we cannot account for the *specialness*, for the *uniqueness* of our friends. Strawson, as I mentioned, denies that narrativity is essential to friendship. He cites the example of Michel de Montaigne who was famous for his exemplary friendship with Etienne de La Boetie, but who was also notorious for his terrible memory:

> Montaigne finds that he is often misjudged and misunderstood, for when he admits that he has a very poor memory people assume that he must suffer from ingratitude: 'they judge my affection by my memory', he comments and are of course quite wrong to do so. A gift for friendship doesn't require any ability to recall past shared experiences in detail, nor any tendency to value them. It is shown in how one is in the present. (Strawson, 2004, 450)

Now, Strawson must be right to suggest that it is more or less possible to act *as a friend would act* in the absence of any memory of past, shared experience. One's best friend* could act towards us with friendliness and affection and *vice-versa*. But that is not, it seems to me, really what is at stake here. Affection should not be judged by memory. But there is more to friendship than affection alone. The question is whether or not it is possible for non-narrative individuals (the 'happy-go-lucky' types as Strawson characterizes them) to comprehend true friendship. I say not, for if it were true that Montaigne really had no memory *at all*, he would be unable to explain why Etienne would matter more to him than Etienne*. He would be unable fully to explain because unable fully to *understand* what was so special about *his* Etienne as opposed to some complete stranger. It is hard not to regard that as a fundamental failure in one's comprehension of friendship.

Now, if this is true of friendship, then it seems to me also true of other special attachments like communal attachments. Deprived of a narrative understanding of the shared life of our community, I would be unable to comprehend the full significance of my attachments to the other members of the association. By abstracting conceptions of community from their temporal context we thus obscure certain salient features of those communities. We lose, in particular, the resources necessary to understand and articulate why it is that these communities should specially matter to those who belong to them. For this reason, I reject the 'happy-go-lucky' view of community implied by Strawson's account. Any adequate vocabulary of community must incorporate an appreciation of temporal extension as reflected in the idea of a shared life. However, it is one thing to claim that community should be conceived in narrative form, quite another to claim that those narratives should be modelled on the structures of journeys. It is to that suggestion I now turn.

Journeys

At first sight, journey narratives might seem an unlikely source of ideas about the structure of community. Journey narratives, as we shall see, very often begin with a painful departure and what appears to be the *breakdown* of community. For example, in *The Pilgrim's Progress*, the narrator relates the following:

> So I saw in my Dream, that the man [Christian, the pilgrim] began to run; Now he had not run far from his own door, but his

wife and children perceiving it, began to cry after him to return: but the man put his fingers in his Ears, and ran on crying, Life, Life, Eternal Life: so he looked not behind him, but fled towards the middle of the plain. (Bunyan, 1984, 9–10)

Embarking on a journey often involves *breaking* communal bonds for the sake of some other (more important) purpose. The journey is thus conceived as a *transition*, as a rejection of and movement away from the corruption or impoverishment of one community and towards the founding of a better community or way of life. This is the interpretation that Michael Walzer has offered of the Exodus story, finding in it a 'paradigm of revolutionary politics' (Walzer, 1985, 7), in which we can identify the rejection of a corrupt society (Egypt), a journey and struggle (through the wilderness), and the founding of a better society (the promised land). Walzer suggests that the 'movement across space is readily reconstructed as a movement from one political regime to another' (Walzer, 1985, 14). The journey, on this view, is distinct from community: it represents the rejection of one community and the struggle towards (though not the realization of) another.

But my argument of the previous section – that we should conceive of communities as *shared lives* – indicates a different way of thinking about the metaphorical significance of the journey narrative. Perhaps the journey narrative *as a whole* can be regarded as analogous to the shared life of a single community. Certainly it is a very widespread, indeed ubiquitous, notion in Western literature that there is a metaphorical correspondence between journeys and lives. Writing of the 'river of life', Jerome K. Jerome explicitly associates journeys with lives (Jerome, 1957, 26). Similarly, in *On the Road* Jack Kerouac has Sal Paradise tell us that 'the road is life' (Kerouac, 1991, 192). Walt Whitman's 'Song of the Open Road' makes the same connection when he writes of the perpetual journey, 'endless as it was beginningless', which, as Janis Stout observes, makes the journey 'coterminous with life' (Whitman, 1990, 127; Stout, 1983, 18). Whitman urges us to 'know the universe itself as a road, as many roads, as roads for travelling souls' (Whitman, 1990, 127).

Journeys in literature are frequently intended to symbolize lives, but why should this be? Why do we so readily associate stories of spatial movement with the stories of our lives? I want to suggest three central reasons. Journeys are readily translated into lives because they emphasize time, change and shape. I shall consider each of these features in turn. First, as Janis Stout explains, journey narratives emphasize the passing of time:

> The effectiveness of the journey as symbolic action largely derives from the facility with which space can become an analogue for time. It is this interchangeability of the two dimensions, spatial and temporal, that is the basic capacity allowing transformation of simple journey narrative into symbolic action. The journey can readily be used as a metaphor for the passage of time or for penetration into different levels of consciousness. (Stout, 1983, 14)

Because the spatial movement of the journey narrative is readily translated into the passage of time, the journey narrative is often used to symbolize the passing of life. *The Pilgrim's Progress* is a clear example here. The story tells of Christian's journey from the 'City of Destruction' to the 'Celestial City' and records the various obstacles that he encounters *en route*. The idea (or part of it) is that the reader is to translate this account of the pilgrim's journey into an account of the life of a Christian. The narrative tells us of the route a pilgrim must take in order to reach the celestial city and clearly symbolizes the way a Christian must live in order to reach heaven.

A second reason for our tendency to associate journeys with lives is that we regard living as a dynamic process. With the passing of time, *things change*. Here, then, the association is less metaphorical and more literal. To travel is to experience and to undergo change. Journeys involve a change of scene. Consider, for example, the dramatic transformation of natural and social environment experienced by Marlow in his journey up the Congo and into the 'heart of darkness'. Journeys can also involve a change of perspective: one's view of the world from a mountaintop is rather different to the view from base-camp. Furthermore, journeys are also very often learning experiences; think of the education Herodotus received from his travel through Egypt. And just as journeys involve constant changes of this nature, so too do lives. Our environment changes as we live, even if we remain in the same place. Seasons change, people come and go, customs and social rituals evolve. The same may be said of our perspective and of our knowledge – that is why Aristotle insisted that the young are unfit to study political science: they are 'not versed in the practical business of life' (Aristotle, 1976, 1094b13–1095a7). And there is an important dialectical element here that is worth emphasizing. Generally when I travel, I move myself, I change myself, but I am also changed by the places I see and those changes in turn affect the moves I choose to make. Equally, we often feel that while we have some control over our lives, we are also to some extent the victims of chance and circumstance. Our lives are our own to live, but 'we are never more (and sometimes less) than the co-authors of our own narratives. Only in fantasy do we live what story we please' (MacIntyre, 1985, 213). Our circumstances affect what we do with our lives, and what we do with our lives affects the circumstances in which we find ourselves.

So, journey narratives are often used to symbolize lives because they convey two important features of a life: time and change. Moreover, and critically, they represent these features in a very particular way. In the journey narrative, movement and change are not completely random and chaotic; they occur within the confines of a unitary structure, a structure provided by the form of the journey. The spatial movement involved in a journey, that is to say, must possess some sort of pattern or *shape* (or some sort of series of patterns or shapes). It must, for instance, be a journey of exploration, homecoming, or indeed home-founding. Movement without this sort of narrative shape is more accurately characterized not as journeying, but as lost (or 'happy-go-lucky') wandering. I think we may say something rather similar about the narratives of lives. In order to be able coherently to narrate a life at all, it must possess some sort of shape that serves to lend intelligibility and continuity to the series of episodes it comprises. As MacIntyre suggests, when 'someone complains – as do some of those who attempt or commit suicide – that his or her life is meaningless, he or she is often and perhaps characteristically complaining that the narrative of their life has become unintelligible to them, that it lacks any point, any movement towards a climax or a *telos*' (MacIntyre, 1985, 217). In this way, journey narratives, like the narratives of lives, combine elements of flux (time and change) with elements of unity (shape).

While, of course, there are limits to the analogy – lives, after all, are quite different from stories (and I shall return to this) – journey narratives can nevertheless help us to appreciate the kinds of shapes that lives can possess. They help us to understand that different lives can be patterned in different ways. And we can appeal to journey narratives to help us to *classify* the shapes of lives. For example, we might say of a particular life that it possesses the shape of a pilgrimage or of an escape or of a quest. Of course these are metaphors again, but they are metaphors which come very naturally to us and which we find highly intuitive when applied to the narratives of lives. It is, for example, a meaningful question to ask whether the life of Frederick Douglass – the African-American slave who escaped to freedom and wrote a narrative of his experience – is most accurately conceived as possessing the shape of an escape, or of a home-founding, or of both, or perhaps of something else altogether.[1]

I have cited three key reasons for thinking it appropriate to associate journey narratives with the narratives of individual lives. Journey narratives convey time, change and shape. I have suggested that the narrative of a life is characterized by these three features and that as a result we find the process of translating between journeys and lives a very intuitive one. All I want now to add to this is the further thought that the narrative of a *shared* journey can similarly be translated into the narrative of a *shared* life. And again, this is a commonplace translation: there are three men (and a dog) in Jerome K. Jerome's boat. The journey up the Thames is a shared journey. And Jerome explicitly suggests that we might learn something about the shared life from his account of the journey:

> How many people, on that voyage [up the river of life], load up the boat till it is in danger of swamping with a store of foolish things which they think essential to the pleasure and comfort of the trip, but which are really only useless lumber. ... It is lumber, man – all lumber! ... Throw the lumber over, man! Let your boat of life be light, packed only with what you need – a homely home and simple pleasures, one or two friends, worth the name, someone to love and someone to love you, a cat, a dog, and a pipe or two, enough to eat and enough to wear, and a little more than enough to drink; for thirst is a dangerous thing. (Jerome, 1957, 26–7)

Shared journeys, like individual journeys, convey the passage of time, involve change, and possess a particular shape or series of shapes. Equally, shared lives, like individual lives, extend through time, encounter change and possess a particular shape or series of shapes. Consequently, it seems to me that, again, we can appeal to journey narratives to help us to understand and to classify the different forms that shared lives can take. It is a sensible question to ask of any shared life, what is its shape? And it may very well be meaningful to answer that the shared life in question possesses the shape of a pilgrimage, an escape, a quest, or even possibly a trip up the Thames.

To summarize, then, my claim so far is that by appealing to the idea of a shared life and by connecting that idea with the narratives of journeys, we can begin to identify a far richer, more open-ended and flexible way of talking about community than currently prevails in much of the literature devoted to the concept. The idea of a shared life helps us to appreciate the possibility that communities might come in a range of different shapes and also to see that it is inappropriate to conceive of a community as a static social entity. But here it might be objected that, for precisely that reason, mine is a very strange way of thinking about community. Traditionally, at least, communities *are* conceived as static associations, as havens of peace, stability and permanence in a potentially chaotic world. That is why journey narratives so often begin with the collapse of community. If it is true that these narratives symbolize time and change, then it seems that they could serve only to *distort* our understanding of communal life, for the whole point of a community, it will be said, is precisely that it is time*less* and that it does *not* change. To this objection I offer two responses. The first is to insist that while communities may be, and often are, conservative, boring, old-fashioned, stifling and oppressive, they are never *static*. As much as their participants might wish that it were otherwise, communities must, for reasons I gave in the previous section, be conceived as temporally extended and they must also change if only because they must interact with the changing world around them.

But still it might be said that the appeal to journey narratives *exaggerates* the changeability of communal life. To this I respond with the words of Ignatieff that I quoted at the beginning of the chapter: 'modern life has *changed* the possibilities of civic solidarity'.

No shared life is truly static, and modernity has ensured that very few come even close. It is true that community is traditionally conceived as a refuge of peace, stability and permanence, but I have already insisted that the traditional conception of community is nearly useless as a response to the modern predicament. If we are to understand the real prospects for liberal community in modern society, we must dispense with the conviction that community is static and adopt instead a vocabulary of belonging that can accommodate the dynamism and flux that modernity has wrought. It is my contention that, precisely because they are coherent and unitary structures that nevertheless emphasize time and change, journey narratives are uniquely placed to provide the sort of vocabulary we need.

Fictions

Let me recap what it is that I think journey narratives contribute to our understanding of political community. In the first and second sections, I suggested that by appealing to the idea of a shared life, we might achieve a richer sense of the special value of community to those who participate in them. In other words, a narrative understanding offers us a clearer sense of what it would be like to live in such a community. In the third section, I suggested that by appealing to journey narratives, we can begin to appreciate the variety of different shapes that shared lives, and hence communities, can take. Already I have betrayed a preference for the use of fictional journey narratives. While I do not want to suggest that factual narratives are at all useless, I do want to argue in this section that fictional narratives are more helpful to the present task.

The stock of stories that constitutes our literary tradition tell us something about the ways in which we have been inclined to understand our lives. The fact that a relatively limited range of narrative structures or shapes has become ubiquitous, recurring constantly in the otherwise very different stories we tell, reveals something rather important I think about the ways in which we understand ourselves. As Walzer has written of the Exodus story, it is 'a big story, one that became part of the cultural consciousness of the West so that a range of political events (different events, but a particular range) have been located and understood within the narrative frame it provides' (Walzer, 1985, 7).[2] Walzer's thought is that in a range of political events (specifically revolutions), we can see the narrative structure of the Exodus reflected (essentially a transition from subjugation to struggle, and from struggle to emancipation). Consequently, his idea is that we may be able to come to a more complete understanding of revolutionary politics by attending directly to the Exodus story. I want to claim something rather similar. My suggestion is that our literary heritage discloses a (small) number of 'big stories' or narrative frames, of which the Exodus is one, that have become part of the cultural consciousness of the West and have thus shaped and been shaped by our ways of thinking about social and political life. And, following Walzer, I want to suggest that by attending directly to the stories and narrative frames that have had this profound effect we might thereby illuminate aspects of our social and political lives that have been obscured by the 'darkening glass' of political theory. The purpose of looking to our stock of fictional stories, then, is that they can help us to identify which narrative shapes are most prevalent and which, therefore, are most likely to shed light on our self-understanding.

There are other reasons for thinking it appropriate to seek such illumination in fictions rather than facts. One commonly cited reason is that fictional narratives provide a richer 'sense of life'. In so far as it is true that journey narratives help us to appreciate what communal life is like, fictions are superior to factual accounts. On the face of it, this may seem a surprising suggestion. How could a made up story shed more light on the experience of human life as it is actually lived than a true story? The problem with factual narratives, I would suggest, is that they are *constrained* by their commitment to truthfulness in this context. That is to say, they are constrained by the author's awareness of the available facts. The author of a fiction is able to tell us exactly what is (and possibly what is not) in a character's mind at any given moment. Frederick Douglass, by contrast, tells us only what he recalls or in some other way discovers. The fact that there is a reality 'out there' to which the author of a factual narrative strives to be faithful means that much of the experience of life of those involved in the narrative will be lost because so much of experience, and especially the experience of others, is necessarily opaque to the observer. Freed from the aspiration to factual truthfulness the author of fiction is able to tell us much more about the inner thoughts of all parties to the narrative.[3] Paradoxically, then, fictional narrative can supply a more realistic and detailed illustration of our lives as we actually experience them than factual narrative.

But it must also be noted that there are limits to this. Philosophers who are sympathetic to the use of literature often emphasize the rich, detailed and complex character of novels. For example, Iris Murdoch argues that philosophy needs 'a renewed sense of the difficulty and complexity of the moral life and the opacity of persons ... It is here that literature is so important ... Through literature we can re-discover a sense of the density of our lives' (Murdoch, 1997a, 294). I have endorsed this kind of claim, but Susan Mendus sounds a note of caution when she suggests that there is also an important sense, often overlooked, in which fictional narratives have a tendency to 'oversimplify'. She explains one respect in which this is so:

> Narratives present the moral and political world 'pre-packaged'; the authority of the text imposes on the reader an understanding of what the moral or political problem is, and a largely shared interpretation of examples which permits only those disagreements for which there is textual warrant. Thus, for example, it is inappropriate to ask whether Raskolnikov was mistaken in thinking that he had murdered Alyona Ivanovna, who survived his assault and was finished off by someone else. The text rules out this possibility and renders the thought of it faintly comic. (Mendus, 1996, 59–60)

As Mendus continues, 'much of the difficulty of moral life is consequent upon the struggle to categorise the kind of situation we find ourselves in' (Mendus, 1996, 60). The problem with literature is that it assumes an answer to that question. It imposes a framework on the moral dilemma, a framework which is so often lacking in real life. John Horton argues that 'texts are characteristically complete and composed, while life is neither – the author describes a situation and there is nothing more to that situation than that which is contained in the text' (Horton, 1996, 83). Factual narratives, of course, do not suffer this defect – it is never certain that the author's interpretation of real events is the right one and there is always more to the situation than that which is contained in the text.

All of this seems to me right. If one hopes to derive from literature a sense of life as we actually experience it, then one should bear in mind the limits to the analogy between literature and life. But to my inquiry, the simplifying tendency of literature is in fact an advantage. I am suggesting that it is precisely because 'much of the difficulty of moral life is consequent upon the struggle to categorise the kind of situation we find ourselves in', that it is useful to our understanding of moral life, and of community life in particular, that we look to fictional journey narratives to provide us with 'complete and composed', 'pre-packaged' shapes by which we may (or may not) be able to make better sense of, or to imagine, our shared lives with our fellow citizens. Fictional journey narratives generally possess a complete and composed structure and shape. Our shared lives, by contrast, can, as I emphasized in the first section, often seem obscure and amorphous. Consequently, my thought is that by appealing to the simplified narrative structures of journeys we may be able to bring these superficially formless relations to life. Following D.Z. Phillips, I appeal to fictions not as a source of *examples* of how we live, but rather as a source of *reminders* of the different ways in which people have conceived of their lives, both individual and shared, in order to illuminate the variety of ways in which we might thus comprehend our own social existence. In the terms of my argument, then, the suggestion is not that we look to fictions to provide examples of how we might share a life in community; the suggestion is that we look to fictions to remind us of the fact that people have often shared lives in a manner quite alien to the way in which contemporary political philosophy often portrays the shared life of a political community. Fictions serve to remind the theorist that conflict need not always be undermining of communal association.

But this claim seems to establish a rather uneasy tension in my argument. My first suggestion was that fictions were superior because they provided complex images of life as it is experienced which incorporate far more of the relevant kind of detail than factual narratives. My second suggestion, however, has been that fictions are superior because they *simplify* life; they provide complete and composed models which can help us to tame the complexity and haziness of our lives as we actually experience them. Well, it might be asked, which one is it to be? Are fictions to be judged superior because of their complexity or because of their simplicity? In fact, I want to claim that the superiority of fictional narratives resides in precisely this tension: fictional narratives are uniquely useful because the images of life they present are both complex in some ways and simple in others. What fictional narratives do, that factual narratives do not, is provide a very rich sense of what life might possibly be like *within* a simplified, complete and composed framework. To be sure, certain possibilities are simply ruled out of the narrative of *Crime and Punishment* and, indeed, are rendered 'faintly comic', but within the simplified and pre-packaged structure, we are offered an eminently rich and detailed characterization of Raskolnikov's predicament. The fact that we are often unclear as to the shape of our lives does not undermine the usefulness of fictional narrative as a tool to help us to appreciate the features of a shared life conceived as conforming to a specific and known shape.

Literature shapes and is shaped by the lives we lead. Certain philosophical tendencies have occluded salient aspects of our lives. My hope is that by attending to literature, we may be able to correct the distortions to our understanding of community that our philosophical heritage has engendered. However, the idea is not to think of fictions as mirrors that directly reflect our lives back to us, but rather to think of them as revealing to us the range of possible forms that a communal life might take and as helping us to appreciate how our lives would be were we to conceive of them as patterned by one or another narrative shape. Given, as I have suggested, that we very often do conceive of our lives as conforming to one or another narrative shape, it seems to me that complete, composed and richly detailed accounts of how these shapes work are invaluable.

But there is a final challenge to my argument here. The most complete, most composed and most richly detailed (fictional) journey narrative will shed no light at all on the communities in which we take ourselves to move, indeed it will only distort them, if that narrative is a work of pure fantasy. Murdoch suggests that it 'may be useful to contrast "fantasy" as bad with "imagination" as good' in literature (Murdoch, 1997b, 11). I think this is important. There is always a real danger that fiction will lapse into fantasy and thereby present us with impossible and inauthentic visions of communal life. We look to fictions for communal imaginaries, not communal fantasies. For this reason, it seems to me that we must always be cautious in our treatment of fiction. It constitutes a powerful resource for the political philosopher, but we should not allow ourselves to be misled by it. For my part, I shall treat the fictional narratives I consider as suggestive, but I shall not let my argument rest solely upon their claims. It might also be worth mentioning here that although it is true that the constant possibility that imagination will give way to fantasy serves to limit the usefulness of fictional narrative, it is not clear to me that this undermines my claim in this section for the superiority in this domain of fiction over fact. Factual accounts are equally exposed to the danger of fantasy: did Frederick Douglass's narrative go exactly as he tells it?

Summary

In this chapter, I have argued that, by suggesting to us different ways of conceiving the shape of a shared life, fictional journey narratives can serve to shed light on the different ways in which we might conceive of a liberal community. This argument provides the method I mean to deploy in the following three chapters. In each chapter, I shall observe how a different journey narrative shape – pilgrimage, escape and quest – suggests a different interpretation of the shape of a shared life and, indeed, of a liberal political community. By consideration of the fictional narratives, I shall seek to articulate the nature and prospects of each interpretation of liberal community. My hope, which I have sought to defend in this chapter, is that by moving to the vocabulary of a shared life, we will be able to begin to rethink the relationship between community and conflict.

3
Community as Pilgrimage

One of the paradigm instances of a community in its conventional sense is the religious community: the congregation. Communities of this kind are structured by their common purposes. Individuals unite in these contexts with those with whom they share a conception of the good, those with whom they share an understanding of what they want their common life to be and to achieve. In the absence of a shared faith, the religious community could not survive. Needless to say, atheists have no place in a religious congregation. Of course this is not to suggest that believers cannot associate with non-believers. The point is just that when we define a religious community as an association of fellow worshippers, atheists are by definition excluded from the communal bond.

Fellow worshippers are liable to be specially concerned for one another and to have a sense of belonging together. These attitudes seem to flow from their shared pursuit of common goods. Their 'deep reason' for associating together is given by their shared religion. Their relationship thus resembles what David Kahane has called an 'object-centred' relationship (Kahane, 1999, 270). Members of the community are related by their shared identification with a common object. As described, the religious congregation constitutes a paradigm instance of community in its conventional sense because of the status it accords to consensus upon fundamental goods and values (though this is not to say that such associations cannot be sites of dissent as well as of consensus). Such communities are purposive associations because their members share the belief that their activity is directed

towards certain positive goals and they share a broad understanding of the nature of those goals. In other words, the
members of the religious community, as I am conceiving it, share
an understanding of what their common activity is *for*. Perhaps,
for example, it is for the realization of a shared life in perfect
submission to the will of God. Consequently, the ideal instantia-
tion of such an association will be one displaying a very high
degree of consensus on the purposes of the community. The
more divided the participants are as to the purposes of their
shared life, the harder it becomes to recognize the association as
a community in this sense at all. In this chapter, I want to
explore this model of community life in some detail and to consider whether or not it can provide a plausible interpretation of a
liberal community.

In other words I want to explore the possibility of making the
structure of a liberal community consistent with our assumptions
about the structure of community in its most conventional sense.
My inquiry is divided into three stages. In the first section, and in
order to get clearer about the character of the shared life of this
sort of traditional community, I shall seek to develop an apparent
structural resemblance between it and journey narratives of pilgrimage. In the second section, I shall consider the questions of
whether and how the pilgrimage shape I have articulated can be
replicated at the level of the liberal state. In so doing, I shall
explain how comprehensive liberal accounts of community, and
specifically that articulated by William Galston, seem in certain
important respects to reflect the pilgrimage shape. Finally, in the
third section, I shall consider whether or not the pilgrimage shape
provides a plausible and appealing interpretation of the shared
life of the members of a liberal society by examining how effectively it responds to the fundamental challenge I have set of
showing how liberal community might survive in conditions of
conflict.

The pilgrimage narrative

It is my contention that in the structure of the religious community
I have described, we can see reflected the narrative structure of a pilgrimage. In this section, I want to develop this claim in some detail.

John Bunyan's *The Pilgrim's Progress* begins with 'The Author's Apology for his Book' which explains that:

> This Book will make a Travailer of thee,
> If by its Counsel thou wilt ruled be;
> It will direct thee to the Holy Land,
> If thou wilt its directions understand (Bunyan, 1984, 6).[1]

Right from the start, the journey is given a determinate end point and purpose: the Holy Land. And this is an important feature of the pilgrimage narrative: pilgrims have a fairly clear idea of where it is that they are going. In his discussion of medieval travel narratives (which, emerging between the 10th and 14th centuries, significantly predate *The Pilgrim's Progress*), Paul Zumthor notes how actual, as opposed to allegorical, tales of pilgrimage possess much the same sort of structure:

> It is a question, in fact, of a *path*, important only by virtue of the holy places that mark the route. The narrative focuses almost exclusively on the ultimate goal, Rome or Santiago de Compostela. In testifying to the experience he has had and to the experience he has lived, the author hopes not only to exalt these sites of grace, but to convince his brothers in faith to imitate him, all the while providing them with the information to facilitate the task. ... He lays out, perhaps without the express desire to so, the road to sainthood (Zumthor, 1994, 810).

Christian's journey in *The Pilgrim's Progress* begins primarily as an *escape* from the City of Destruction at which point Christian knows only that he must 'Fly from the wrath to come'; he knows 'not whither to go' (Bunyan, 1984, 9). But if that were the whole story, if Christian's journey were simply a *flight*, it would not have the shape of a pilgrimage. Some sort of destination is required. As Philip Edwards has explained, the 'one cannot be without the other; journey as escape can have a Christian meaning only if a final destination is known and sought. ... The concept of pilgrimage shifts the emphasis of the journey from the departure to the destination' (Edwards, 1980, 112–13). And sure enough, slightly later in the text, a destination emerges when Christian declares that 'I am come from the City of *Destruction*, and am going to Mount *Zion*' (Bunyan, 1984, 38).

There are several important features of the idea of the destination in pilgrimage narratives. First, it is important that the destination be known with a fairly high degree of certainty. For example, it is entirely meaningful for a person to think of himself as embarking on a pilgrimage to the Kaaba in Mecca. It would be very peculiar, however, for a person to think merely that she was embarking on a pilgrimage *away from here*, having no concrete idea of the destination whatsoever. Even to think of oneself as embarking on a pilgrimage to *somewhere* in South-West Asia seems inadequate. Part of what it is to be a pilgrim is to be going somewhere really quite specific. Also, to be a pilgrim is to have a fairly comprehensive grasp of the nature and significance of the destination. It would be very strange for a person to say that he was embarking on a pilgrimage to the Kaaba, but that he had absolutely no idea why, no idea of what the Kaaba was or of why it was an important thing for him to visit. Of such a person, we would be tempted to say that he was not really embarking on a *pilgrimage* at all. Connectedly, and this is a slightly harder quality to articulate, the destination must not be trivial; it must be perceived as sacred or exalted. The importance of this condition is that it serves to distinguish the pilgrim from certain other kinds of traveller such as the 'tourist'.[2] Clearly there is a difference between the person who travels to Mecca because doing so represents a central pillar of his religion and the person who travels to Mecca simply in order to take photographs of the pretty mosques, a person who might just as happily have travelled to Europe instead in order to take photographs of the pretty cathedrals.[3]

And we can recognize that the destination in *The Pilgrim's Progress* satisfies these conditions: Christian knows exactly where he should be going, he knows why he should be going there, and his reasons for going there are not trivial to him. He is engaged in a pilgrimage. Now, of course, *The Pilgrim's Progress* is not intended simply as a journey narrative, it is intended to describe the narrative of a certain kind of life. The good life, according to Bunyan, is not a life spent languishing in the City of Destruction, but rather a life spent on the road to the 'Celestial City'. The good life is the life of a Christian. In other words, the good life has the shape of a pilgrimage. One whose life possesses this shape will know with some degree of specificity where her life is (or should be) going, she will grasp in some detail the nature of her goals, and she will regard those goals as sacred. Note that there is no implication here that such a life will be easy or straightforward. The Pilgrim knows where he or she is going, but not necessarily how to get there. And, in any case, there will be dangers, temptations and challenges to confront *en route*: 'the slow of dispond', 'Mr. Worldly-Wiseman', 'The Valley of the Shadow of Death' etc. A successful pilgrimage is by no means assured and could certainly be a fragile achievement.

What implications does the pilgrimage narrative have for the shape of a *shared* life? Centrally, it seems to suggest that it will be a life spent in pursuit of a common goal. If you and I set out in pursuit of the same shrine, which we both value for the same reasons, then we may, like Christian, Faithful and Hopeful in *The Pilgrim's Progress*, consider ourselves fellow pilgrims. Notice how this fellowship resembles the kind of bond described in Plato's ideal community, to which I alluded in Chapter 1, of family members who have everything in common. Indeed, the fact that Christian's fellow pilgrims are named after Christian virtues suggests that we are not really to think of them as separate persons at all: Faithful and Hopeful are not separate *individuals*; they are the qualities and dispositions that a Christian will need in order to bring his pilgrimage to a successful conclusion. The distinction between individual and collective is thus thoroughly blurred, even dissolved, in Bunyan's narrative. The participants in this kind of shared life are essentially of a common mind. There is very little disagreement to be observed between fellow pilgrims.

However, not all pilgrimage narratives are of quite this form. Consider the case of the Canterbury pilgrims in Chaucer's *The Canterbury Tales*. The Canterbury pilgrims are a notably motley assortment. Knights, millers, monks, nuns, Oxford scholars, wives, and many others besides are represented among the party. It is clearly part of the point of the narrative to stress the rich diversity of the group. Furthermore, Chaucer's pilgrims are most certainly not of a common mind like Bunyan's pilgrims. Think for example of the bickering between the Miller and the Reeve or of the 'marriage debate' provoked by the Wife of Bath, five times married and insistent that God never specified the number of times that a woman may be wed (Chaucer, 1985, 219). As the narrator observes, 'Folk of all kinds, met in accidental / Companionship, for they were pilgrims all' (Chaucer, 1985, 1). The only thing holding the Canterbury pilgrims together is their shared pilgrimage. But now this is important: for all of their very many differences, the Canterbury pilgrims still share in the pursuit of a common goal and a common good: 'from all the shires / Of England, to Canterbury they come, / The holy blessed martyr there to seek, / Who gave his help to them when they were sick' (Chaucer, 1985, 1). The pilgrims are united by the fact that they are all going to Canterbury seeking the 'holy blessed martyr' (St. Thomas à Becket). Note how the fellowship here resembles the bond of Aristotelian friendship: the Canterbury pilgrims share in the pursuit of a common object. There is no requirement here that the pilgrims be of a common mind in any stronger sense. The difference between Bunyan's and Chaucer's views of the fellowship of Pilgrims thus resembles the difference between Plato's and Aristotle's views of community which I discussed in Chapter 1.[4] Whilst Bunyan suggests the need for (almost) complete consensus between pilgrims, Chaucer recognizes that part of the good of the pilgrimage depends upon a degree of personal separateness between pilgrims: the Canterbury pilgrims are enriched by their wealth of divergent experiences whilst Bunyan's pilgrims seem terribly solemn by comparison. However, both Bunyan and Chaucer are united in thinking that in order to be counted fellow pilgrims at all, the participants in the journey must share an understanding of the nature and value of the destination. Whether they are enriched or not by their differences, the only reason the Canterbury pilgrims come together is that they are going to the same place. They would never otherwise have associated with one another. Nevertheless, Chaucer's narrative demonstrates the important point that there is room in the pilgrimage narrative for the possibility of disagreement between pilgrims: I might think that the best way for us to get to the Kaaba is by plane, you might think we would be better off on foot. I may think it legitimate to be married as many times as I like whilst you may think differently. These kinds of disagreements need not be in any way undermining of the fellowship of pilgrims, in fact they can often enhance the fellowship.

There is even room, it seems to me, for more fundamental disagreements about the nature and value of the destination. Perhaps I am a Sunni Muslim whilst you are Shia. In this case, it seems to me that our shared journey may, in some cases at least, still be deemed a pilgrimage by fellow pilgrims, but that the extent of our fellowship would be more limited than were we to hold precisely the same conception of our destination. Of course, if I were travelling to Mecca because doing so represented a central pillar of my religion and you were travelling there to take photographs of the pretty mosques, it would be very odd to regard our shared journey as a pilgrimage. To be sure, it might be true that we both regarded our respective journeys as pilgrimages, but they would be different pilgrimages and we would not be fellow pilgrims. The central point is that the greater the disagreement about the destination becomes, the more attenuated the sense in which ours is a shared pilgrimage becomes.

In summary, then, the shape of a shared life suggested by the pilgrimage narrative is that of a life spent moving towards a common goal upon the nature and value of which fellow pilgrims agree. This does not, however, preclude disagreement between pilgrims. Pilgrims may be of a common mind like Christian, Faithful and Hopeful, but they need not be. The Canterbury Pilgrims are not of a common mind, yet their fellowship remains strong. That said, there is a limit to how much disagreement the pilgrimage narrative can tolerate whilst still remaining a story of pilgrimage. Perhaps, I have suggested, the shared journey of a Sunni and a Shia Muslim to Mecca might still be counted a pilgrimage, but the shared journey of a Muslim and an enthusiastic photographer would surely not.

The connection between the pilgrimage narrative shape and the vision of community I outlined above should by now be quite clear, but allow me briefly to join the dots. The conventional view of community, as exemplified by the religious congregation, is a community grounded in (Aristotelian) 'object-centred' relationship and consensus. The narrower the consensus, the weaker the friendship and the weaker the friendship, the more attenuated the community will be. The shared life of such a community will be one dedicated to the pursuit of the common good of its members. I have suggested that such a shared life may be thought of as possessing the shape of a pilgrimage. The individual life of the pilgrim is one dedicated to the pursuit of a specific good, and where pilgrims agree upon the good they pursue, we may consider them to be fellow pilgrims. The shared life of such fellow pilgrims will be one dedicated to the pursuit of a common good antecedently known: the particular shrine of which they share an understanding, for instance the Celestial City in Bunyan's narrative and the Holy Blessed Martyr in Chaucer's tales. The more minimal the shared understanding of the shrine pursued, the weaker their fellowship becomes, and the more attenuated their shared pilgrimage becomes. Both the conception of community as consensus and the pilgrimage narrative embody a shared recognition and pursuit of a good. I shall now consider the possibility that the shared life of the members of a liberal polity could be conceived as possessing the shape of a pilgrimage.

Liberal community as pilgrimage

I have suggested that we can see stories of pilgrimage reflected in the shared lives of traditional communities. The question I want now to consider, though, is whether this conception of community, which I shall term the pilgrimage model of association, can plausibly account for the value of community within a liberal framework. At first sight, it certainly seems that it cannot. The pilgrimage model conceives of community as stemming from the shared pursuit of a very specific, religious ideal. Even allowing for the diversity apparent in Chaucer's narrative, it seems hard to reconcile the idea of pilgrimage with the pluralistic character of the modern liberal polity. It is far from clear that we share in the pursuit of any common ideal, let alone a religious one. This is just the kind of community that Rawls insisted we must abandon, a community understood as 'a political society united in affirming the same comprehensive doctrine.' Rawls is clear that this 'possibility is excluded by the fact of reasonable pluralism together with the rejection of the oppressive use of state power to overcome it' (Rawls, 1996, 146). On Rawls's view, it would be illiberal to think of the liberal polity as an association dedicated to the shared pursuit of common goods.

But not all liberal theorists share this view. 'Comprehensive' liberals argue that the liberal state either should, or necessarily does presuppose a comprehensive conception of the good and that we should or must therefore think of the liberal community as a sharing in the pursuit of that good. In other words, these liberals hold that it is entirely possible or even necessary to conceive of liberal community on the pilgrimage model. In this section, I want to consider one such account of liberal community, articulated by William Galston. In his book, *Liberal Purposes*, Galston defends liberalism against its anti-liberal (and, specifically, communitarian) critics by arguing that the debate is 'poorly framed', that it is not necessary for us to pick sides in the manner that is often implied by those involved. Modernity is not as morally bankrupt as the likes of MacIntyre suggest, and the liberal state is not as morally neutral as liberals like Rawls would like to think. Galston counsels the adoption of a 'third way: a nonneutral, substantive liberalism committed to its own distinctive conception of the good, broadly (though not boundlessly) respectful of diversity, and supported by its own canon of the virtues' (Galston, 1991, 44). The focus of Galston's positive argument is on the articulation of a liberal conception of the good which can serve to provide content to a catalogue of liberal virtues and an ideal conception of liberal character. In short, he hopes to reveal an ensemble of ethically substantial 'liberal purposes' that 'define what the members of a liberal community must have in common' (Galston, 1991, 3).

In this way, Galston identifies his understanding of liberal community squarely with the pilgrimage model of association that I have articulated. The liberal state is a purposive association; it is a neo-Aristotelian community conceived as a sharing in the pursuit of common liberal purposes or goods which provide 'the unity that undergirds liberal diversity' (Galston, 1991, 3). And the task of articulating a common liberal good is a critically important response to 'the centrifugal forces of diversity. *E pluribus unum* is not merely a geographical and institutional but also a cultural and moral imperative' (Galston, 1991, 10). In the absence of a shared conception of the liberal good, there will be no liberal community, and the liberal state would be reduced to a mere *modus vivendi*: 'a raw and shifting balance of contending social forces' (Galston, 1991, 3). So, Galston's claim, like that of many other comprehensive liberals, is that community can be explained within a liberal framework by providing a comprehensive account of the liberal good upon which liberal citizens might converge notwithstanding their disagreements and differences. In this way, community and conflict are reconciled.

For the reasons I have already given, this enterprise is liable to arouse immediate suspicion. The members of liberal societies do not

conceive of themselves as sharing in the pursuit of a good in anything like the same way as, say, a religious community. Even if
Galston were right that such a sense of community is a necessary
precondition of the liberal state's stability, it is far from clear that it
is practically attainable within a genuinely liberal context. But this
might be a bit quick: we can surely to some extent separate the *form*
of the pilgrimage narrative from its *content*. The key feature of the
narrative structure is that the association of fellow pilgrims is established and animated by their shared destination. While it is true
that in the narratives I have considered, the destination has been a
very specific destination of religious significance, I do not think that
that feature is essential to the broader narrative form. As I suggested
in the previous section, the pilgrimage narrative form suggests a
shared life structured around the shared pursuit of a common good
of some kind. And it seems to me that we can identify something of
this nature in Galston's argument: he articulates an account of the
good liberal society and conceives of the liberal community as an
association engaged in the pursuit of that ideal. Perhaps it is possible to conceive of the shared good of the liberal polity in such a
way as to render it more hospitable to pluralism.

Galston stresses that the liberal purposes, upon which the unity
of the liberal state is to be based, leave considerable room for diversity. The idea is that while the liberal conception of the good is ethically substantial, it does not go as far as to suggest that there is a
single way of life valid for all (Galston, 1991, 181–2). Consensus on
the liberal good does not require complete consensus on all moral
matters. Instead, Galston's liberalism reflects what he terms 'a kind
of minimal perfectionism' (Galston, 1991, 299). In this respect his
vision is clearly less demanding than the conception of the good
that unites the members of certain religious communities. While a
religious community would generally allow space for its members
to pursue different activities and trades, the room for moral variety
would be much more constrained. By contrast, Galston anticipates
a liberal community displaying a significant degree of moral
conflict. His concern is not to eliminate such conflict, but rather to
articulate a core set of shared understandings which would serve to
offset and temper any tendencies to disintegration. 'The resulting
scope for disagreement and diversity is considerable indeed'
(Galston, 1991, 182). So, in this way Galston hopes to reconcile the

liberal commitment to freedom, and hence diversity, with the unity of a traditional community.

In order to see exactly how this is supposed to work, let us take a closer look at Galston's account of the liberal good. Galston suggests that his vision of the good emerges principally as a corollary of a common human understanding of the bad. He suggests that we 'can agree that death, wanton cruelty, slavery, poverty, malnutrition, vulnerability, and humiliation are bad without having a fully articulated unitary account of the good' (Galston, 1991, 168). This seems right; Galston's list of evils places very few constraints upon the kind of life a person may legitimately live. Of course there will be some who do not endorse the evils he describes. Galston acknowledges that his *summum malum* will not be acceptable to all, but argues that we need not be detained unduly by this fact. He appeals to Aristotle's observation that we cannot expect the same kind of precision in our study of moral and political life as we can in the study of mathematics and logic (Galston, 1991, 169). A conception of the good (or bad) may, in this view, be regarded as a legitimate political tool as long as it holds in general and for the most part. Universal assent is neither necessary, nor realistically to be expected.

So, on the basis of this *summum malum*, Galston formulates a list of seven dimensions of the liberal conception of the human good: life – 'life itself is good and ... the taking or premature cessation of life is bad'; normal development of basic capacities – basic capacities here are taken to include 'the senses, various kinds of physical motion, speech, reason and sociability'; fulfilment of interests and purposes – it is good for individuals to form, act upon and achieve their goals; freedom – valued both instrumentally and intrinsically; rationality – an ability to understand, to respond to and deploy rationality in the association of means and ends, relations with others and public deliberation; society – a recognition of the intrinsic value of social relationships; and subjective satisfaction – while 'it is better to be Socrates dissatisfied than a pig satisfied, it is also better, *ceteris paribus*, to be Socrates satisfied than Socrates dissatisfied' (Galston, 1991, 174–6).

It is worth pausing just to emphasize that Galston does not mean to suggest that these values are to be regarded as direct corollaries of the evils from which he begins. For example, his conception of freedom, which he suggests is to be understood as 'noncoercion'

(Galston, 1991, 175), does not follow directly from a commitment to the badness of slavery – unless we were to give to the term 'slavery' an implausibly broad definition. Clearly it would not be at all inconsistent to regard chattel slavery as an absolute evil whilst acknowledging the legitimacy, and even goodness, of various other forms of coercion. The point I mean to stress here is that Galston's account of the liberal good is, as he acknowledges, clearly a comprehensive account. Nevertheless, it is also relatively parsimonious and leaves room for a considerable degree of moral diversity.

Convergence on Galston's account of human well-being provides the basis for his liberal political community. His idea is that the shared pursuit of the liberal good will engender a sense of belonging together among citizens recognizing that they are part of a co-operative endeavour 'to create and sustain circumstances within which individuals may pursue – and to the greatest possible extent achieve – their good' (Galston, 1991, 183). The understanding that one is involved in such a collaborative endeavour will promote the recognition, by citizens, of various special obligations to one another and will encourage them to cultivate and display various liberal virtues. The neo-Aristotelian character of the account is quite clear. By articulating and promoting a comprehensive liberal conception of the good, Galston supposes that the liberal polity will foster 'object-centred' attachments among citizens. Attachments, that is to say, that are explained by reference to the shared purposes and goals of those involved.

We can also now see more clearly the way in which the shared life of such a liberal community possesses the shape of a pilgrimage. In both the comprehensive liberal community and the pilgrimage narrative, the collective are conceived as a group united by their shared pursuit of a particular goal. In Galston's case, that goal is the liberal good; for the Canterbury pilgrims, that goal is the shrine in Canterbury. The community's purpose, like the pilgrims' purpose, is relatively clearly defined and specified in advance. Galston's liberal community is not directed towards some vague or uncertain goal; it is directed towards the fulfilment of the seven dimensions of liberal well-being. And just as a person who does not value the pilgrimage's object is not to be considered a fellow pilgrim, a person who does not value the liberal conception of the good is not to be considered a full member of the liberal community. Such people will need to be coerced if they are to share fully in the life of the polity. This is perhaps easier to see if we turn briefly to the variant of comprehensive liberalism defended by Stephen Macedo. Macedo suggests that his brand of liberalism 'holds out the promise, or the threat, of making all the world like California. By encouraging tolerance or even sympathy for a wide array of lifestyles and eccentricities, liberalism creates a community in which it is possible to decide that next week I might quit my career in banking, leave my wife and children, and join a Buddhist cult' (Macedo, 1990, 278). What I am suggesting, then, is that we might think of the parties to Macedo's liberal community as being engaged in a pilgrimage to a society like California. They all agree from the outset that they would most like to live in such a society, and so together they strive to realize and perfect that society. The story of their shared life is a story of their striving to achieve the liberal ideal upon the nature of which they antecedently agree. As Chaucer's pilgrims strive to reach Canterbury, liberal pilgrims strive to reach (or rather to realize) the 'celestial city' of San Francisco.

In this section, I have sketched one way in which it seems we might hope to reconcile the value of community with the permanence of pluralism. Galston's minimal perfectionist account appears to provide a way of realizing community within a liberal framework by appeal to the pilgrimage model of a shared life. Essentially, the idea is that agreement on the liberal conception of the good can serve to make fellow pilgrims of liberal citizens. Their shared pursuit of that good – their shared pilgrimage – generates the sense of integration and of belonging together which I have associated with the idea of community. The question I want now to consider is that of whether it really works. Does the pilgrimage model, so understood, provide an adequate interpretation of the liberal political community?

Assessing the pilgrimage model

One reason for doubting the adequacy of the pilgrimage model of liberal political community concerns its apparent exclusiveness. Macedo's exaltation of the 'California dream' is a particularly provocative example here. While some people would certainly thrive in the environment he envisages, there would also doubtless be many who would feel extremely uneasy and out of place.[5] This is some-thing that the comprehensive liberal readily acknowledges: 'certain types will find the liberal culture hospitable (artiste, entrepreneur, arguer, and playboy) and others (devout and simple) will find the going tough' (Macedo, 1990, 62–3). While Galston's account of the liberal good leaves a considerable amount of room for diversity – more, he insists, than Macedo's – it is by no means infinitely inclu-sive: 'it will not, and cannot, satisfy everyone' (Galston, 1991, 301). In and of itself of course, accepting this is no hardship. I have already noted Galston's observation that it would be too demanding to expect universal consensus in moral affairs. That a liberal com-munity will not include absolutely everyone is hardly surprising and does nothing to undermine the attractiveness of the pilgrimage model. For example, it is fairly safe to assume that neo-Nazis would take issue with a number of the dimensions of Galston's account of human well-being and, consequently, would fall outside of the liberal community. Few would consider this a great loss; most would consider it a virtue. There is nothing in principle wrong with an exclusionary community. Indeed, we may well think that it could scarcely be otherwise.

The problem relates to where (and how) exactly we draw the line between insiders and outsiders. If it were only extremists who were excluded from the liberal community, then perhaps there would be no cause for alarm. But the pilgrimage model seems rather less inclusive than that. For a start, Galston recognizes that his account of the good life will rule out certain varieties of belief including secular nihilism, theological withdrawalism, moral monism, Nietzschean irrationalism, and barbarism (understood as deliberate or heedless deprivations of minimal goods) (Galston, 1991, 177). This list is in fact clearly quite extensive and threatens to rule out a large number of ways of life; it is not only the neo-Nazis who are going to find life hard in the comprehensive liberal state. Part-icularly troubling is the exclusion of moral monism. It is notorious that a significant portion of the US religious right hold that there is only one God and indeed only one corresponding morality; moral monism is very far from being the proclivity of a small minority. It is important to note that by saying that such beliefs are 'ruled out' Galston does not mean that believers will be excluded from society, just that their beliefs 'cannot be used as the basis of public action'

(Galston, 1991, 177). Nevertheless, this does seem to imply that such believers will have no place in the liberal *community*. They will not be excluded from the liberal polity, but they will not identify with it in the same way as a person who endorsed the liberal good because they will not see their purposes reflected in those of the community.

Another worrying exclusion from Galston's liberal community is suggested by his second dimension of human well-being, the normal development of human capacities. This he fleshes out as follows:

> Normal members of the human species are endowed with certain basic capacities: the senses, various kinds of physical motion, speech, reason, and sociability, among others. We regard it as good to be born with normal basic capacities, and we regard it as a serious misfortune when infants are born with defective capacities relative to that norm (Galston, 1991, 174).

This seems a particularly contentious component of Galston's account of the liberal good. It is well-known that many deaf parents have been inclined to prefer that their children be born deaf so as to enable them to share fully in the deaf culture and community.[6] On Galston's account we are to regard it as a serious misfortune for a child to be born deaf. Positively to celebrate the occurrence would, from the perspective of the liberal good, be downright corrupt. It seems that alongside the neo-Nazis and barbarians we can place a great many deaf parents, safely beyond the liberal community.

This might seem a cheap shot. After all, Galston is clear that there is 'nothing hard and fast' about his account of the liberal good. It would be easy enough to refine the account so as more adequately to capture the 'intuitions about well-being that underlie liberal social orders' (Galston, 1991, 173). I am sure that this is right, but I am not clear that it helps a great deal. In so far as we define community as the shared pursuit of a comprehensive good, there will always be awkward exclusions in a society characterized by a plurality of comprehensive conceptions of the good. Suppose that we did refine Galston's characterization of normal basic capacities such as to remove the requirement to regard deafness in children born to deaf parents as a serious misfortune. Clearly that would prove equally, if not more, controversial: there are a great many people who would endorse Galston's initial formulation; it *is* corrupt to celebrate deafness in a newborn child. Of course, the tempting solution here is simply to remove the development of normal basic capacities from Galston's specification of the liberal good altogether. It is too controversial and so cannot provide a component of the shared understanding that unites liberal citizens. But clearly this is not a particularly satisfactory solution from Galston's point of view, because it undermines his general strategy. He wants to suggest that we can unite around a relatively *comprehensive* conception of the good. Any moves to make that conception of the good less comprehensive are necessarily going to be unwelcome, for on the pilgrimage model they will be detrimental to social unity. But this is my point: Galston is surely right to suggest that there are some understandings about the good that are widely shared by liberal citizens. Some of them may even be quite comprehensive. However, any attempt to conceive of liberal community as the shared pursuit of a comprehensive liberal ideal is necessarily going to be exclusionary. And, importantly, it is not only going to be the obnoxious extremists who will find themselves beyond the pale.

So the pilgrimage model suggests a significantly exclusionary conception of liberal community. But why should this be thought to constitute a defect of the account? Well, it reveals that the pilgrimage model provides an inadequate solution to my initial puzzle. The task is to show how liberal solidarity could emerge and survive in conditions of conflict. Galston's account of liberal community fails to do this. He provides a coherent account of liberal political community, but one which comes only at the cost of excluding a not insignificant section of the population who are unable to endorse the liberal conception of the good. The key problem here is that you have to be a comprehensive liberal in order to have a place in Galston's liberal community and, as I have sought to suggest, not everybody who participates in the liberal society is a comprehensive liberal. As a result, Galston's account seems to bypass a central political problem (even *the* central political problem) facing modern democratic societies of how they are to accommodate significant, and seemingly permanent, illiberal minorities within a broadly liberal framework. If the task were to account for liberal community among those already committed to a comprehensive conception of the liberal good, Galston's argument would serve very well. But that, I have suggested, is not really the problem at all. The real and urgent task is to reconcile community with the genuine, and deep, moral conflict that seems to constitute a permanent feature of modern liberal democracy. With regard to that task, the pilgrimage model fares rather poorly.

Galston might respond here by pointing out that liberal community on the pilgrimage model is something that would need to be fostered. Of course it is true that not everybody *right now* would endorse his account of liberal well-being, but that is precisely why he stresses the importance of civic education. Galston defends a fairly robust conception of civic education directed towards 'the formation of individuals who can effectively conduct their lives within, and support, their political community' (Galston, 1991, 243). The idea, then, could be that over several generations the inhabitants of the liberal state will become progressively 'liberalized' and, as a result, will feel increasingly at home in the liberal community. But again, this does not solve the problem of reconciling community and conflict. Rather, it accounts for community only by *reducing* conflict. And, for the reasons Rawls has given, that is something about which the genuine liberal will rightfully feel uneasy. Galston acknowledges that 'few individuals will come to embrace the core commitments of liberal society through a process of rational inquiry. If children are to be brought to accept these commitments as valid and binding, the method must be a pedagogy that is far more rhetorical than rational' (Galston, 1991, 244). This line of argument seems to veer dangerously close to what Rawls describes as oppression.

The worry is that, given the conditions of modernity and specifically the fact of pluralism, Galston's account of political community seems theoretically unattractive. As Andrew Mason has suggested, comprehensive accounts of liberal community necessarily generate what he terms 'extrinsic conflict' with communities below the level of the liberal state:

> *Extrinsic* conflict in my sense can be of different kinds. It occurs whenever a community or its current way of life has the causal effect of undermining the existence *or* current way of life of another community, or whenever promoting or protecting a community or a current way of life has that effect (Mason, 2000, 72).

By upholding and promoting the comprehensive conception of the liberal good through the processes of civic education, the comprehensive liberal community will necessarily, and quite deliberately, affect the way of life of certain communities below the level of the state. As Galston clearly asserts, in cases of conflict, the 'civic core takes priority over individual or group commitments (even the demands of conscience), and the state may legitimately use coercive mechanisms to enforce this priority' (Galston, 1991, 256). What is unclear here is from where the legitimacy of coercion is supposed to derive. Presumably, it must be from the objective goodness of the liberal ideal, but that goodness, as Galston acknowledges, is unlikely to be reached as the outcome of the process of rational inquiry. In other words, coercion of those who do not endorse the civic core is justified by appeal to what is effectively an article of faith. It is thus unsurprising that comprehensive liberals are often charged with cultural imperialism, 'of seeking to impose their culturally specific values whilst claiming falsely that these principles are universally valid' (Mason, 2000, 72).

And it is important to emphasize that this is not just a problem of Galston's particular variant of comprehensive liberalism. The problem is a structural inevitability in any comprehensive conception of community. It is an issue, that is to say, that will arise in any shared life possessing the shape of a pilgrimage. In pluralistic contexts such associations are necessarily exclusive. The only means by which they may come to accommodate a larger number is by reducing the content of the civic core or by reducing pluralism. If we take the former option, our comprehensive liberalism loses its claim to comprehensiveness, if we take the latter option, we will have to involve ourselves in the arguably illiberal practice of fostering consensus.

There is another, and rather deeper, problem with the pilgrimage model that casts its appropriateness as a response to the task I have set of identifying the sources of solidarity in a divided society even further into doubt. I want to suggest that the pilgrimage model of community is *structurally confining*. We can see this most clearly by returning for a moment to the pilgrimage narrative. The goal of Christian's journey is specified, and specified in quite some detail, right from the very beginning. In order to embark on a pilgrimage, I must *already* have decided where it is that I want to go. To this extent, then, the pilgrimage narrative structure is, from the outset, a 'closed' structure. There is no scope for the pilgrim to change his mind about the destination. If he did change his mind, then he would cease to be a pilgrim, or at least he would become a different kind of pilgrim.

Much the same I think is true of Galston's conception of liberal community. Galston specifies the dimensions of the liberal good in advance, in order to structure the shared life of liberal citizens. The liberal good is not something discovered or created in and through the shared life on the pilgrimage model. It is first formulated in theory, and then pursued in practice. Once again there is no scope for participants in the community to change their minds about the purposes of their association. Because the goals of the community are theorized in advance, the shared life takes on a closed structure; it is scripted ahead of time.

The problem is that this view of community implies a rather peculiar view of the shape of a life. As Susan Mendus has observed:

> It is only rather unusual lives which are correctly characterized as lives led in pursuit of a specific and constant aim. For most of us, aims change consequent upon earlier decisions, and what I deem to be in my interest is, in part, a function of choices I have made and decisions I have taken along the way. (Mendus, 2002, 150)

Most reflective people proceed not by formulating their good and then pursuing it, but rather in a manner closer to that described by Stuart Hampshire when he suggests that while 'I live, my conception of good and evil naturally and normally tends to be revised and amplified as my experience and my reflection may suggest. Precisely because my values and goals are guiding my activities and sentiments as my life proceeds, my reflections on virtues and values are kept open, ready for the new evidences of experience' (Hampshire, 1999, 67). It seems to me that much the same applies to the way in which we normally think about the shared life. As reflective people, we want to think of our shared future as open, open to the possibility of revision in the light of experience.

So, here is a rather serious problem for the pilgrimage model of liberal community. Its closed structure is liable to be experienced by many as confining. Even if I entirely endorsed Galston's seven dimensions of the liberal good, it would be perfectly intelligible for me to feel uncomfortable and confined by the idea that the shared life of my political community would be a life directed towards the pursuit of those goals, towards the realization of a society like California. Sure, I might endorse those purposes now, and perhaps I will still endorse them when I die, but that does not mean that I want them to *dictate* the shape of my life or of the life I share with my fellow citizens. It seems to me that an acceptable account of a genuinely liberal community would have to be one the shared life of which is open-ended and not structurally confining in the manner of the pilgrimage model.

Perhaps it would be tempting for the comprehensive liberal like Galston to argue at this point that I have rather misrepresented his position. Perhaps he would agree that it certainly would be confining to 'pre-script' the goals of the liberal community in the manner of the pilgrimage model, but yet deny that there is any need for us to take such a stringent view of the comprehensive liberal community. Why could we not regard the liberal purposes that shaped our shared life as values and goals open to revision in the light of experience? It seems to me that we could not because Galston is quite clear that his liberal purposes (or something like them) are supposed to provide stable 'sources of commonality' among the members of the liberal association (Galston, 2002, 78); they are to provide the 'unity that undergirds liberal diversity' (Galston, 1991, 3). If we accept that liberal purposes will shift and evolve over time, then it is not clear how they could provide the kind of unity and stability that Galston seeks. Certainly, the shared life of such an association would no longer possess the shape of a pilgrimage.[7]

So, I have identified two significant problems with the pilgrimage model of liberal community. First, it seems that it may be unacceptably exclusionary and secondly, it seems that it may be structurally confining. Both of these problems are troubling because they appear to subvert the liberal credentials of the community (at least on certain interpretations of the liberal enterprise) and also to undermine its appropriateness as a response to the task, which I have suggested is fundamental, of reconciling community and permanent conflict. Of course, and as we have seen, the comprehensive liberal may not deny any of this. Her claim need not be (although it often is) that the pilgrimage model of association provides an *ideal* way of reconciling community and pluralism; her claim may rather be that it is the *only* way of reconciling the two. In other words, if we want liberal community and the political stability that comes with that, we will have to accept the need for some (significant) measure of exclusion and confinement. Community is forged at liberty's expense.

Summary

In this chapter, I have considered the merits of a conception of liberal community that is structured so as to render it continuous with more traditional understandings of community life as instantiated, for example, in certain traditional religious communities. I began with the image of such a community as an 'object-centred' association, an association, that is to say, explained by reference to the common goods pursued by its members. I proceeded to suggest that in this image of communal life it was possible to see reflected the narrative structure of a pilgrimage. Fellow pilgrims are united by their shared pursuit of a specific destination; theirs too is an object-centred relationship. And the pilgrimage narrative shape suggests a more abstract structure by which we might understand the shared life of a community as the shared pursuit of a particular end or good.

Next, I considered the question of whether the pilgrimage narrative shape could provide a plausible structure for the narrative of the shared life of the members of a liberal community. I appealed to William Galston's comprehensive liberalism in order to show that, in principle at least, it is possible to reconcile the shared pursuit of a common good with a considerable degree of moral diversity. However, I proceeded to argue that a community so conceived is problematical, particularly from a *liberal* standpoint. There are two reasons for this. First, a conception of liberal community that generates such a high degree of exclusion provides a rather unsatisfactory response to the problem I have set of accounting for liberal solidarity in conditions of pronounced conflict. At the limit, the pilgrimage model invites the charge of cultural imperialism. Secondly, and in many ways more troubling, I have suggested that the pilgrimage model might constitute a structurally unacceptable shape for a liberal community. Because the model stipulates the goals of the community in advance, it closes off the future and is liable to be experienced as confining by those who recognize that their values and goals evolve and change in the light of experience. It might seem, then, that the narrative shape of an acceptable account of liberal community has to be more open-ended than the pilgrimage structure can allow.

Of course, some theorists, as we have seen, choose to end their inquiries at this point. Either they side with the likes of Galston and suggest that significant exclusions and a degree of confinement are an inevitable cost of community that we must bear; or, alternatively, they side with the likes of Rawls and suggest that, because significant exclusions are an inevitable cost of community, we must abandon the hope of a liberal community in any substantial sense. I want to press on, however, and explore the possibility, illuminated by the appeal to journey narratives, that there are other ways of understanding liberal community for which significant exclusions and structural confinement are not an inevitable cost. Certainly the form of my argument may be thought to provide a ground for hope here. For it may be that just as there is more than one way of conceiving of the structure of a journey, there may also be more than one way of conceiving of the structure of a liberal association that realizes the values of community while also acknowledging the permanence of pluralism and indeed of conflict.

4
Community as Escape

> A grocer excavating the ruins of his store, handing tins of
> soup and milk to those who wanted them, and saying quite
> solemnly, 'Put it on the account'; a pub standing drinks out
> of hours to the local raid victims; a manager staying on late
> at the factory so as to give a lift in his car to weary work-
> men – such things were unknown before September 1940;
> and after June 1945. Neighbours forgot their censorious
> rivalries and joined together in impromptu parties to fight
> fires, to repair each other's houses, to look after children, to
> cook meals. Life, briefly, seemed more important than
> money (Calder, 1969, 178).

As Brian Barry has observed, 'The Second World War was an ex-
cellent creator of a sense of solidarity, since everyone shared in
the danger of defeat, and the blitz created a genuinely common
hazard' (Barry, 1996, 128). The 'spirit of the blitz' describes a
sense of community arising from a sense of shared fate. This kind
of community has in common with the traditional religious community I discussed at the beginning of the previous chapter the
fact that it is bound by what we might term 'object-centred' relationships. Relationships defined, that is to say, by appeal to a
common understanding or purpose. However, in this case, the
object upon which the relationship is centred is not a comprehensive conception of the common good, symbolized by the pilgrim's
shrine, but rather a common bad or a common evil. Specifically,
the object upon which these relationships are centred is the blitz.

A further difference is that the life of this sort of association is (obviously) not shaped by a shared *pursuit* of the common evil; on the contrary, it is shaped by a shared *resistance* or *evasion* of the common threat.

In other words, then, the spirit of the blitz suggests a kind of inverted, negative version of the comprehensive traditional community I considered in the previous chapter. While the unity of the traditional religious community was expressed in its members' shared understanding of what their communal life was *for*, the unity of the blitz community was expressed in its members' shared understanding of what their communal life was *against*. And it seems to me that we can make a similar claim about the latter's structure. Because the community is conceived through its resistance to a common hazard, we can infer that it must presuppose both that there *exists* a common hazard, like the blitz, and that the participants in the association all agree that the common hazard is *genuinely hazardous*. Clearly, a person who insisted that there was nothing to fear from the German bombing, who sincerely believed that the war constituted no sort of danger at all, could not be expected to share in the spirit of the blitz and would fall outside of the community it characterized. In this chapter I want to explore this model of community life and to consider whether or not it can provide a plausible interpretation of a liberal community in conditions of conflict.

I shall follow a similar structure to that of the previous chapter and proceed in three stages. In the first section, and in order to get clearer about the form of the shared life suggested by the spirit of the blitz, I shall seek to develop an apparent structural resemblance between it and journey narratives of escape. In particular I shall focus on the escape narrative of Richard Adams's *Watership Down*. In the second section, I shall consider the questions of whether and how the escape shape I have articulated can be replicated at the level of the liberal state. In so doing, I shall explain how what I shall term 'negative' liberal accounts of community, traces of which can be found in the doctrine that has become known as 'the liberalism of fear', seem in certain important respects to reflect the escape shape. Finally, in the third section, I shall consider whether or not the escape model provides a plausible and appealing interpretation of the shared life of the members of a liberal society by examining how effectively it responds to the fundamental challenge I have set of realizing community in a pluralistic context.

The escape narrative

I believe that in the structure of the blitz community I have described, we can see reflected the narrative structure of an escape. In this section, I want to develop this claim in some detail. Richard Adams's *Watership Down* tells the tale of the escape of a group of rabbits from the warren in which they had grown up when it is threatened by the arrival of property developers wishing to construct 'high class modern residences' on the land (Adams, 1974, 20). The story begins with a note of alarm and a dire warning when Fiver tells Hazel that they must leave:

> 'Hazel – the danger, the bad thing. It hasn't gone away. It's here – all round us. Don't tell me to forget about it and go to sleep. We've got to go away before it's too late.'
> 'Go away? From here, you mean? From the warren?'
> 'Yes. Very soon. It doesn't matter where.'
> 'Just you and I?'
> 'No, everyone.' (Adams, 1974, 21)

In stark contrast to the pilgrimage narratives I considered in the previous chapter, there is no notion here of where the journey is supposed to lead to. It 'doesn't matter' where the rabbits go. For the time being at least, they need to be anywhere other than *here*. Note, also, the inclusiveness of the warning: 'everyone' must go because everyone is at risk. In other words, the parties to an escape, unlike the parties to a pilgrimage, do not need to have any particular, shared idea of where it is they are going. The focus of the escape narrative is provided not by the journey's destination, but instead by its origin.

There are a number of important features of the idea of the origin in escape narratives that it is worth pausing to emphasize. First of all, the origin must be perceived as being in some way bad or corrupt, for otherwise there would be no sense in the idea of escaping from it. Of course, in *Watership Down*, the warren itself is not regarded as especially corrupt. The escape's origin is provided instead by the imminent arrival of property developers, sensed by Fiver, who would destroy the warren and kill its occupants. So, in order for a journey of escape to begin, there must be some reason for escapees to want to escape. Secondly, and connectedly, the origin must be perceived as sufficiently threatening or evil to provoke flight. The imminent arrival of property developers could not serve as a cause for escape if the rabbits were willing to put up with any threat that they felt it posed. Thirdly, the origin has to be quite specific. Here again is a commonality between escape and pilgrimage. Just as pilgrims must have some fairly specific idea of where they are going, escapees must have some fairly specific idea of what they are fleeing. Of course the foe may be rather vague and amorphous; for Fiver, it is simply 'the bad thing'. But nevertheless it seems that it must have some substantial content, for otherwise it would be unclear as to exactly *how* the journey undertaken by the escapees constituted an escape at all. For example, I must have at least some notion of where the threat emanates from, for if I did not, how would I know in which direction I ought to run? How would I know that I should *run* at all? If I did not know where the enemy was and, perhaps, how exactly it threatened me, why would I imagine that my running in, say, a Westerly direction should constitute an escape from it?

So it is the origin that provides the escape narrative with its focus and structure. A group of rabbits, those convinced by Fiver's prophecy, leave the endangered warren and embark on a journey the destination of which is, initially at least, extremely unclear. But it would not be true to say that the escape has no destination whatsoever. Indeed, it seems to be a structural necessity of the escape narrative that escapees have at least some inkling of where they will go. The primary concern of the rabbits is certainly negative: to escape from danger. But the question of where exactly they are escaping *to* lingers in the background and becomes increasingly pressing as the danger recedes. They are not happy to escape to just anywhere as demonstrated by their refusal to live in Efrafa – a rival warren bearing an uncanny resemblance to a totalitarian police state (Adams, 1974, 237–50).

The escaping rabbits are not simply running for their lives; they are running for a particular *kind* of life. There is no time for them to dwell on this positive vision, but it does exist. The general point I mean to emphasize here is that there are in fact two perspectives we can take on the escape narrative. We can, and typically do, view such journeys as movements away from x, where x is some clear and present evil. But excessive concentration on the evil to be avoided can often cause us to overlook the fact that the journey is also (*must also be*) a movement towards y. Of course, y will generally be rather vague and underdetermined, but it is nevertheless important not to forget that in order to be able to escape the worst, you must have some idea of what could count as better, and presumably some hope that it really exists. And we can see this in *Watership Down* when Fiver reveals that he does in fact have some idea of where the rabbits are trying to get to: 'I know what we ought to be looking for – a high, lonely place with dry soil, where rabbits can see and hear all round and men hardly ever come' (Adams, 1974, 45). The rabbit's escape does have a destination, but note that it is a destination without any determinate substance. It is a space defined by what it lacks. It is not so much a *good* place as a *safe* place.

We are now in a position to summarize the escape narrative structure. Escapes are journeys which are structured by and primarily focused upon their origin which is conceived as some fairly substantial evil or threat that must be evaded or otherwise resisted. The journey constitutes a movement away from the evil. And the precise character and direction of the journey is largely determined by the dangers that inspire it. However, that does not mean that the escape is a journey without end or purpose. Just as it can be understood as a movement away from something terrible, it can also be understood as a movement towards something better. To be sure, the 'something better' pursued is liable to be very vague and insubstantial, but it is something.

It is possible for us to discern in this kind of narrative structure an image of the shape of an individual's life. The escape narrative suggests a life without a strong sense of positive purpose, but with a very keen sense of a negative threat to be resisted. A person possessing this sort of life would not so much be *pulled* forward by her ideals and ambitions as *driven* forward by her fears. Lives possessing this kind of shape are perhaps more commonplace among the poor and oppressed than they are among the rich and the affluent. For the deprived, choices of job, behaviour, lifestyle and so on are dictated primarily by the need to survive in a tolerable fashion, to escape the horrors of abject poverty and persecution. Of course this is not to say that the poor do not have grand ideals and ambitions, only that they are less able to allow their lives to be shaped by those ideals and ambitions. The hopes that do shape their lives are liable to be rather more modest and insubstantial: the hope for food, clothing and shelter for instance. The privileged, by contrast, need worry less about such things and often allow their lives to be shaped by more substantial desires and dreams.

The escape narrative also yields a vision of the shape of a shared life. The escape described in *Watership Down* is, from the outset, a collective undertaking. But, once again, it is not an undertaking characterized by a strong sense of positive purpose. The participants in a shared life possessing the shape of an escape need not conceive of themselves as sharing in the pursuit of a substantial common goal. Instead, their common life is structured by their keen sense of sharing a substantial common fate. Such a life is not pulled forward by the attraction of some shining ideal, but driven by the shared fears of the collective. Consequently, the scope for disagreement among those who share such a life is very considerable. Not only may the participants disagree about the best way of responding to the evil that threatens them; they may also disagree about where exactly their shared life is to lead them. There is no sense here that fellow escapees must, like some fellow pilgrims, be of a common mind. The coherence of the shared life requires only that the parties to it agree upon the nature of the threat.

We can now see the way in which the escape narrative is reflected in the 'spirit of the blitz' which I described at the beginning of the chapter. The citizens united by the blitz were not united by a common goal. They were not in any substantial agreement about where they wanted their society to go. There was no shining ideal in the pursuit of which they shared. Their unity was defined instead by a common enemy that threatened them all. Doubtless there were substantial disagreements between those united by the blitz, but it was precisely that which made the phenomenon so remarkable; 'censorious rivalries' were swept aside. The fact that people disagreed about the good life became completely irrelevant against a backdrop of German bombs. There were more important things to think about. What mattered most was finding a means of escape from the hazard that the blitz presented. And in that task almost all were united. But, again, it would be a mistake to imagine that these people pursued no common goals whatsoever. They sought to construct a safer society, a society less troubled by the air raid siren. Such a goal was clearly a relatively insubstantial goal, but it was a goal nevertheless. And it provided a ground for hope.

However, there may also seem to be a certain awkwardness and disanalogy here. There is something rather peculiar about describing Londoners united in the face of the blitz as 'escapees'. On the contrary, it might be said, these people chose to stay on in the city, bravely to confront the threat when they could (or some of them could) easily have fled to safer parts of the UK. The idea of escape might be thought to imply flight and cowardice, notions which seem out of place here. Indeed it is tempting to say that escape was the last thing on the minds of many Londoners during the war. But it seems to me that this concern rests on an unhelpfully narrow characterization of escape. Escape need not imply *evasion*. Escaping from something will very often involve confronting it. Consider, for example, the way in which Frederick Douglass's escape from slavery involves a pivotal confrontation with the slave-breaker, Mr. Covey (Douglass, 1999, 67–8). Even more strongly, it seems to me that we can properly describe as being, in some sense, an escapee the person who actively embarks on a *crusade* to root out the evil in question. My point is that escape, as I understand it, can take many forms and need not imply either flight or cowardice. The defining feature of the escape narrative, as I understand it, is its focus upon the negative – and the desire to be free of the negative – as the motivating element. So understood, it seems not implausible to regard the spirit of the blitz as conforming to the escape pattern. I shall now consider the possibility that the shared life of the members of a liberal polity could be conceived as possessing the shape of an escape.

Liberal community as escape

I have suggested that narratives of escape imply a particular vision of the shared life and, hence, a particular vision of community. The escape model of community is the model of a *negative* community, a community defined chiefly by the things it opposes and resists rather than the things it values and pursues. We can see this kind of negative community realized in the spirit of the blitz where the constant, and largely indiscriminate, threat of death brought (most of) the population of London together in an unprecedented display of solidarity and communal warmth. The question I want now to consider is whether this idea of negative community could be replicated at the level of the liberal polity. Could the escape model provide a plausible interpretation of liberal political community?

On the face of it the signs are not good. The spirit of the blitz emerged only because Londoners were confronted by the unmistakeably clear and imminent threat of violent and premature death. As I suggested of the escape narrative, the origin must be sufficiently threatening to provoke flight. It is just not clear that in the normal course of events, we can identify any threat so severe as to provoke among liberal citizens anything approaching the level of solidarity that was witnessed during the blitz. As Brian Barry observes:

> That disasters, natural or manmade, stimulate social solidarity is one of the best documented findings in social science. But what is equally well-established is that after things return to normal, solidarity gradually diminishes. I simply do not think that our society could be transformed by acceptable means into one displaying solidarity of an intensity sufficient to support a generously-funded system of welfare benefits. (Barry, 1989, 195)

It may thus seem that to realize the required sort of community at the level of the liberal state, it would be necessary to sustain a constant, and suspiciously illiberal, state of alert and fear among citizens. This suggests a rather less palatable perspective on the escape model of community. Samuel Scheffler makes the important, and disconcerting, point that 'even relatively decent governments may find it irresistible at times to use fear as a way of deflecting criticism or deflating political opposition. A judiciously administered dose of alarm can do wonders in inducing a compliant frame of mind and encouraging people to rally round their leaders' (Scheffler, 2006, 14). As such, the escape model may seem to provide a rather unsatisfactory model for liberal community.

But again it could be helpful here to distinguish form and content. I have suggested that the structure of a negative community is that of a community united by the bad things it opposes rather than the good things it pursues. Perhaps the 'bad things' which provide the community's focus need not be either natural or manmade disasters, but rather more everyday vulnerabilities and fears. Perhaps the community's focus could be upon something like the list of negatives suggested by William Galston, which I noted in the last chapter: 'death, wanton cruelty, slavery, poverty, malnutrition, vulnerability, and humiliation' (Galston, 1991, 168). By appealing back to our animal nature, we may identify a range of hazards to which we are all clearly vulnerable. As Alasdair MacIntyre has written, we 'human beings are vulnerable to many kinds of affliction and most of us are at some time afflicted by serious ills. ... [Our] lives are characteristically marked by longer or shorter periods of injury, illness or other disablement and some among us are disabled for their entire lives' (MacIntyre, 1999, 1). Might it be possible to interpret liberal political community as an association structured by its resistance of evils such as these, an association the shared life of which is shaped by a recognition of the common, human vulnerabilities of its members?

This is a vision of human sociality famously portrayed in Shakespeare's *King Lear*. Cast out of the Royal household and into the stormy night of the heath, Lear is confronted by Edgar, disguised as a beggar, and glimpses a stark truth, which Michael Ignatieff describes as the 'final equality of basic need' (Ignatieff, 1984, 42): 'Thou art the thing itself; unaccommodated man is no more but such a poor, bare, forked animal as thou art' (Shakespeare, 1975, Act III, Scene 4). In this equality of wretchedness, Lear recognizes a communal bond which pays no heed to class and status and tears off his clothes. As Marshall Berman suggests, 'Shakespeare is telling us that the dreadful naked reality of the "unaccommodated" man is the point from which accommodation must be made, the only ground on which real community can grow' (Berman, 1983, 108). But this is a vision of community that has not figured heavily in liberal political philosophy. The 'major political philosophies of the past several decades' have, on the whole, been 'philosophies of prosperity, preoccupied with the development of norms for regulating stable and affluent societies' (Scheffler, 2006, 3). As I suggested, escape-shaped lives are more prevalent among the dispossessed. It can be easy to miss the 'poor, bare, forked animals' when they are draped in the finery of Western affluence.

Nevertheless, there is a strand in recent political philosophy which has stressed the primacy of the negative, of fear, cruelty and human vulnerability. The seminal statement of this position is provided by Judith Shklar in her articulation of the doctrine she termed the 'liberalism of fear'. The liberalism of fear constitutes an 'entirely nonutopian' interpretation of the liberal project (Shklar, 1989, 26). It holds that 'the basic units of political life are not discursive and reflective persons, nor friends and enemies, nor patriotic soldier-citizens, nor energetic litigants, but the weak and the powerful. And the freedom it wishes to secure is freedom from the abuse of power and the intimidation of the defenceless that this difference invites.' What this form of liberalism centrally requires is 'the possibility of making the evil of cruelty and fear the basic norm of its political practices and prescriptions.' The fundamental goal is one of 'damage control': to avoid or reduce the great evils of cruelty and fear (Shklar, 1989, 27–30).[1] The doctrine emphasizes the reality of absolute evil and the inevitability of perpetual conflict about the good life and consequently insists that we surrender our concern for political ideals and utopias in order to focus instead on securing a minimally safe and decent society. Somewhere 'someone is being tortured right now' Shklar provocatively asserts (Shklar, 1989, 27); our political philosophy can do no other than make this appalling reality its first priority. Our concern should be for the establishment of primary freedoms, basic toleration and minimal decency in our treatment of one another. Everything else can and must be deferred.

The liberalism of fear clearly reflects the structure of the escape narrative as I set it out in the previous section. Like the group of escaping rabbits in Adams's novel, the negative liberal polity does not pursue any particular political 'destination'; it does not, as Shklar puts it 'offer a *summum bonum* toward which all political agents should strive.' But, she continues, 'it certainly does begin with a *summum malum*, which all of us know and would avoid if only we could' (Shklar, 1989, 29). Parties to the liberalism of fear do not engage in discussion about where their society is going ('the more exhilarating but less urgent forms of liberal thought' (Shklar, 1989, 38)), they focus on escaping an evil the reality of which they all recognize. This brand of liberalism assumes that 'the proper business of politics, as Hobbes perceived, is protection against the perennial evils of human life – physical suffering, the destructions and mutilations of war, poverty and starvation, enslavement and humil-iation' (Hampshire, 1999, 8–9). Unlike many of the prevailing Western political philosophies, the liberalism of fear begins from an image of humans as not so very far removed from the terrified rabbits of *Watership Down*, 'poor, bare, forked animals' all, exposed and vulnerable to the cold harsh elements of modern life. In both the escape narrative and the liberalism of fear there is a degree of urgency, generally prompted by some clear and present danger or vulnerability, which operates to discourage extended political contemplation of the good life.

It might seem rather odd to suggest that in the liberalism of fear we can find a distinctive interpretation of a liberal community. Advocates of the kind of 'negative liberalism' defended by Shklar have typically sought to distance themselves from the discussion of community. Shklar asserts that communitarian longings 'cannot even arise' until the institutions of primary freedom are in place (Shklar, 1989, 35–6). She insists that the concern for communal belonging is simply not a *political* concern:

> To seek emotional and personal development in the bosom of a community or in romantic self-expression is a choice open to cit-izens in liberal societies. Both, however, are apolitical impulses and wholly self-oriented, which at best distract us from the main task of politics when they are presented as political doctrines, and at worst can, under unfortunate circumstances, seriously damage liberal practices. (Shklar, 1989, 36)

The message seems to be that while community is an entirely legit-imate concern for the members of a privileged liberal society, it is a potentially dangerous distraction for the liberal political philo-sopher. There are more important things for us to think about (somebody somewhere is being tortured right now). We should defer the task of theorizing community until we have achieved at least a minimal level of security and freedom.

But what the escape narrative suggests to us is that community is not as readily separable from the achievement of basic security and freedom as Shklar's account seems to imply. Consequently, and crucially, the escape narrative indicates that it may be possible to achieve community even in the conditions characterized by the liberalism of fear. Think again about *Watership Down*. Clearly the rabbits do not forsake community; theirs is a cooperative undertaking. They work together as a team, and their ability to do so is critical to the success or failure of their enterprise. Consider the episode of 'the crossing' in which the rabbits must cross a river in order to escape a dog running loose in the woods (Adams, 1974, 44–50). Two of the rabbits, Fiver and Pipkin, are weak and agitated and are incapable of swimming across the river and Hazel, effectively the leader, is at a loss as to what they should do. Blackberry, the cleverest rabbit, suggests that they sit on a piece of wood, which could then be pushed across the river by another rabbit. Unfortunately, Blackberry is not strong enough to push the wooden platform himself and he lacks authority, so at first his plan is ignored:

> 'Who's strong?' said Blackberry. 'Bigwig! Silver! Push it out!'
> No one obeyed him. All squatted, puzzled and uncertain.
> (Adams, 1974, 48)

In order to get things moving it is necessary for Hazel, the rabbit with authority, to issue an order. But neither Blackberry nor Hazel is strong enough to push the platform alone, so it is necessary for the stronger rabbits – Bigwig and Silver – to assist. In other words, then, the crossing (the escape from the dog) succeeds only as a result of the cooperation of several of the rabbits. Adams is very careful to emphasize this point, and similar situations arise again and again throughout the story. The sense of community among the rabbits, their willingness to cooperate together and to make sacrifices for one another, is no dangerous distraction; on the contrary, it is critical to the escape's success.

From this perspective, it seems that it may be a mistake for the liberalism of fear to forsake community. It is a commonplace that there is strength in numbers and it is not at all implausible to think that we are more likely to succeed in our effort to resist evil and minimize fear where we work together. What the case of *Watership Down* suggests is that it is unnecessary to appeal to the (apolitical) value of personal and emotional development through communal belonging in order to vindicate the political value of community. The political task set by the liberalism of fear seems to require that we be willing and able to pool our skills and resources (we will need strong people, clever people, authoritative people). It is not enough that the parties to a fearful liberalism endorse a minimal toleration and live-and-let-live attitude; they must cooperate in a common project. Poor, bare, forked animals cannot survive long alone. As MacIntyre observes, vulnerability breeds dependence: it is 'most often to others that we owe our survival, let alone our flourishing, as we encounter bodily illness and injury, inadequate nutrition, mental defect and disturbance, and human aggression and neglect' (MacIntyre, 1999, 1). In short, to emphasize the negative is to reveal just how much we need each other. Human beings 'actually feel a common and shared identity in the basic fraternity of hunger, thirst, cold, exhaustion, loneliness or sexual passion. The possibility of human solidarity rests on this idea of natural human identity' (Ignatieff, 1984, 28).

This is a striking conclusion. On its face, the liberalism of fear seems an extremely minimalist doctrine which presents itself as being highly suspicious of the idea of political community. But I have suggested that in fact the doctrine contains within itself a powerful and distinctive account of community. It suggests the possibility that a sense of political community might be anchored not in some elusive conception of the common good, but instead in our all too obviously shared vulnerabilities and fears. By beginning from a vision of humans as the poor, bare, forked animals they are, we are able to identify a set of common, fundamental political concerns which can potentially serve to provide shape to the shared lives of liberal citizens. I shall now consider whether this is an adequate account. Does the escape model, so understood, provide a satisfactory interpretation of a liberal political community?

Assessing the escape model

On the face of it, at least, the escape model seems to provide a more promising account of liberal community than the pilgrimage model I discussed in Chapter 3. I found the pilgrimage model wanting on grounds of its exclusivity. Because it conceived community as the shared pursuit of an ideal – the liberal good – it was unable to account for a sense of community that extended to those with whom the agent disagreed, to those who did not endorse the liberal good. I argued that this marked a defect of the account because the key task facing the advocate of liberal community is to show how a sense of belonging together with one's fellow citizens might coexist with pronounced conflict about the good life. In this respect it seems that the escape model fares considerably better. As I have suggested, there is no requirement that either the parties to an escape, or the parties to a fearful liberalism should share a conception of the good, even one as parsimonious as that articulated by Galston. The negative, escape-shaped model of community is centred on a shared conception of the bad. Fearful liberal citizens have a sense of belonging together because they feel a common and shared identity in the basic fraternity of vulnerability and fear. Because agreement on the bad is much more widespread than agreement on the good, this makes for a far more inclusive account of political community.

Moreover, the escape model of liberal community seems also to overcome the other objection I levelled against the pilgrimage model. As I have indicated, the escape model is (relatively) open-ended; it makes no attempt to pre-script the positive goals of the community – it does not specify a *summum bonum* towards which the members of the community are supposed to be striving. In this way, it seems to allow the positive shape of the community to evolve and change in the light of experience and thereby avoids the charge of structural confinement that I associated with the pilgrimage shape.

Barry raised the objection that disaster presented a rather unpredictable and unstable basis for community. What, after all, are we to do when things return to normal? But I think this worry is surmountable. Part of the point of the liberalism of fear is to encourage us to think harder about what is actually meant by 'normal'. As Bernard Williams has written, 'one thing that the liberalism of fear does is to remind people of what they have got and how it might go away' (Williams, 2005, 60). Disasters may come and go, but things have certainly not returned to 'normal' if by normal we mean a world free from vulnerability. The fearful liberal is 'conscious that nothing is safe, that the task is never-ending' (Williams, 2005, 61). What becomes evident as the story of *Watership Down* proceeds is that the escape is not in fact a flight from one specific, and momentary, threat – that posed by the property developers – but an ongoing engagement against 'The Thousand' enemies of rabbits, an engagement which the rabbits can expect to persist for as long they remain the vulnerable animals they are (Adams, 1974, 16). This can also help us to respond to Barry's concern that there is something rather unpalatable about a community sustained by fear. The fact that catastrophes of various forms stimulate negative community, he remarks, 'should hardly lead us to welcome an increase in solidarity created by war or natural disaster' (Barry, 1996, 128). But I have suggested that it is not necessary to conceive of negative community in this way. It is possible to articulate a far more appealing account of negative liberal community by grounding it in the sense of shared fate fuelled by the recognition of our common, human vulnerabilities. Of course this remains a negative image of community, but it is a considerably less nihilistic image than that suggested by Barry.

The idea of negative community, so understood, also seems to provide a plausible interpretation of the practices of mutuality that I have suggested we can identify in modern democratic societies. I observed that one striking feature of the practice of trust was that it revealed the degree to which the members of modern societies depended on one another. As I mentioned at the time, one of the reasons that trust is so important to us is that 'we cannot single-handedly either create or sustain' many of the things that we value most (Baier, 1994, 101). The escape model renders the prevalence of trust in the liberal community intelligible by tracing it to the frailty and vulnerability of solitary individuals. We are all creatures who need others in order to make our lives tolerable and to pursue the things we value *whatever those things may be*. By beginning from the idea of humans as mutually dependent, fearful animals, it becomes much easier to understand the ubiquity of trust among them than it is where we begin from a more conventional image of liberal man as self-sufficient and independent.[2]

We may likewise regard the prevalence of mutual concern in modern society as traceable to a shared recognition of human vulnerabilities. We all bleed, so we give blood. We regard healthcare and a certain level of education as among the basic conditions of any tolerable life, so we pay taxes to fund those services. Many of the kindnesses we do for one another seem to stem not from our concern to promote each other's good, but rather from our concern to resist the ills that afflict us all. Indeed, in so far as we do act to promote one another's 'good', the claim that our actions constitute an instance of kindness and concern becomes rather more dubious. For example, it is relatively uncontroversial that the social provision of healthcare and education, justified by appeal to the centrality of such things to any tolerable life, constitutes an expression of concern. It is much more controversial to suggest that the public regulation of the nation's diet and exercise, justified by appeal to the suggestion that a healthy diet and exercise are conducive to our good, constitutes an expression of concern. We more typically regard such initiatives as expressions of paternalism. Similarly, it is one thing for you to donate your blood to me on the grounds that I need it; that I regard as an expression of genuine concern. It is quite another thing for you to buy me opera tickets on the grounds that my good is better served by 'culture' than by computer games; that I regard as an unwelcome and patronizing intrusion on my lifestyle. Indeed, even if I believed that you were probably right that my good would be better served in that way, I would still be tempted to resent your 'interference' in my affairs. My point here is that most of the least controversial forms of concern and kindness we display towards our fellow citizens are most plausibly and agreeably understood by reference not to the goods we pursue, but to the ills we resist.

Our sense of belonging together is also explicable through the escape model. The sense of belonging together shared by escapees is shaped not primarily by their common identity or purposes, but rather by their common predicament; it is shaped by what they resist and not by what they pursue. This seems a plausible interpretation of the sense of belonging we can witness in modern societies. Consider, for example, Jerome K. Jerome's articulation of belonging in the modern city:

> We are creatures of the sun, we men and women. We love light and life. That is why we crowd into the towns and cities, and the country grows more deserted every year. In the sunlight – in the daytime, when Nature is alive and busy all around us, we like the open hillsides and the deep woods well enough: but in the night, when our Mother Earth has gone to sleep, and left us waking, oh! The world seems so lonesome, and we get frightened, like children in a silent house. Then we sit and sob, and long for the gas-lit streets, and the sound of human voices, and the

answering throb of human life. We feel so helpless and so little in
the great stillness, when the dark trees rustle in the night wind.
There are so many ghosts about, and their silent sighs make us
feel so sad. Let us gather together in the great cities, and light
huge bonfires of a million gas-jets, and shout and sing together
and feel brave. (Jerome, 1957, 56)

Here belonging is conceived not positively, as the shared pursuit of
a common ideal, but negatively, as the shared resistance of solitude
and loneliness. On this view, we experience a sense of belonging
with our fellow citizens because we can never forget that, beneath
our diverse and clashing garments, we are all poor, bare, forked
animals who fear a lonesome world devoid of human contact and
support.

So far, then, so good. The escape model seems to provide an
appealing and plausible interpretation of community in a pluralistic
context. By shifting the deep commonality upon which the community is based from a commonality with respect to the good to the
commonality of a shared fate, the escape shape seems to provide a
(relatively) non-comprehensive source of liberal solidarity and integration. But I believe that there is, nevertheless, a problem with the
escape model. We can see this by returning to a point I made about
the escape narrative in the first section. There is a question, always
lingering in the back of an escapee's mind: 'where are we going to?'
As I have suggested, a journey of escape has to be going *somewhere*.
The question of the journey's positive direction cannot simply be
ignored. We can observe something similar of an escape-shaped
community. The liberalism of fear endeavours to deliver us from
evil, but where exactly does it deliver us *to*? As Michael Walzer has
written, the liberalism of fear can be conceived as a bulwark against
evil, but 'a bulwark and its defenders stand in front of something.
What is it that they are defending? On behalf of what are we fearful'
(Walzer, 1996, 18)? The idea of a negative community focuses our
attention on the ills to be resisted, but to ignore the community's
positive face is to provide only a partial account of the association.
People who see only the evils, hazards and ills that confront them,
people who have no idea of what could possibly constitute a better
existence, have no reason to escape. Indeed, the very idea of escape
would be incomprehensible to them. The fact that the negative

liberal community is understood as an association that *resists* evils entails that the association is not a refuge of the utterly hopeless. As Jonathan Allen argues, 'a defensive liberalism requires an understanding of the way of life it is committed to defending' (Allen, 2001, 344). In order to provide a complete account of the negative community I have articulated in this chapter, we need to be able to say something about its positive face.

But herein lies the problem. It is not at all clear just *what* we are supposed to say at this point. How are we to account for the positive face of the liberal community conceived on the escape model? One possible answer is provided by the idea of escape in *Watership Down*. Viewed from one direction, the rabbits' journey is an escape from their enemies; that is the negative face of their enterprise. Viewed from the other direction, however, theirs is a journey to a place from which enemies are absent, Fiver's high, 'lonely hills, where the wind and the sound carry and the ground's as dry as straw in a barn' (Adams, 1974, 63). On this account, the positive face of the community is to be understood as essentially the direct corollary of its negative face. If, that is to say, the liberal community is conceived as an association structured around its resistance to cruelty, suffering and various forms of vulnerability, then we might say that its positive face, the goal for which it is striving, is a life *free* from cruelty, suffering and those various forms of vulnerability. But that will not do. It would be inaccurate to suggest that a complete account of liberal community could be provided merely by appeal to the evils it resists and their positive corollaries. As Allen remarks, if our goal is, 'as Shklar suggests it should be, to protect individual lives from cruel and arbitrary power, why does this lead to a *liberalism* of fear – or indeed to any particular political doctrine? After all, if our concern is primarily or exclusively for physical security, then why not settle for Leviathan and a quiet life' (Allen, 2001, 344–5). Walzer concludes that when we defend the bulwarks, 'we are usually defending something more than our lives; we are defending our way of life' (Walzer, 1996, 18). Whatever it may be that we are defending behind the bulwarks, it seems that it must be something more than the high and lonely hills of Watership Down.

The central problem here is that a shared resistance to common ills is insufficient to distinguish a specifically *liberal* community. Just about *any* community, including highly illiberal ones, could be described in these negative terms. Consider, for example, the Mafia communities of Hollywood legend. Clearly those communities sought to protect their members from certain forms of fear, cruelty and vulnerability, and they displayed the sorts of practices of mutuality I described in the Introduction, but they were anything but liberal. While the escape model successfully accounts for the basic, and necessary, practices of a liberal community, it does not account for whatever else the liberal community is. It does not account, that is to say, for whatever it is that makes the liberal community a distinctly *liberal* community.

To provide a complete account of liberal community, we need a more positive story than the escape model can by itself supply:

> the liberalism of fear depends upon what we might call the liberalism of hope. I don't mean this in any sentimental way but quite literally: what we are afraid of is that the things we have come to value, our accomplishments until now, and our plans for the future will be destroyed by violent men. When we defend the bulwarks, then, we are committing ourselves to an ongoing engagement and a pattern of activity. For what the bulwarks are meant to defend doesn't exist naturally, has to be made, and isn't finished. (Walzer, 1996, 19)

If it is to provide an acceptable account of liberal community, the liberalism of fear needs a liberalism of hope and, as Bernard Williams has suggested, that leaves us with the rather awkward question of 'what, and how much' we are justified in hoping for (Williams, 2002, 308). Just how hopeful can the liberalism of hope be? An obvious answer here, for those with high hopes, would be to flesh out the positive face of the escape by appeal to the idea of pilgrimage. Structurally, that approach seems to work. Viewed from one direction, Christian's journey, in *The Pilgrim's Progress*, is a journey of escape from the City of Destruction; that is its negative face. Viewed from the other direction, of course, it is a pilgrimage to the Celestial City. On this account, the positive face of the community is considerably more than a direct corollary of its negative face. Clearly, this is precisely the image of community advocated by William Galston that I discussed in the previous chapter. Viewed from one direction, Galston's liberal community reflects an escape from 'death, wanton cruelty, slavery, poverty, malnutrition, vulnerability, and humiliation' (Galston, 1991, 168). Viewed from the other direction, it reflects a pilgrimage to the liberal ideal. Structurally, this is coherent, but it will not do. While Galston's account does succeed in differentiating the liberal community from any number of other non-liberal communities, I argued at length that it was too positive; it was too exclusive and structurally confining to provide an acceptable interpretation of the shared communal life of a diverse liberal society. Whatever it is we are building behind the bulwarks of a fearful liberal society, it is not the Celestial City.

Clearly, then, this leaves us in something of a bind. The escape model provides a plausible account of the negative face of the liberal community, but it seems incapable of providing a complete account, as it fails to do justice to the positive face of our shared life. Ultimately, it is too negative. For this reason, we need to allow for the possibility that the shared life of the members of a liberal polity might merge from an escape into a different, and less negative, narrative shape. But this requirement, I have suggested, generates a new problem. The narrative shape into which the escape merges cannot be as positive as a pilgrimage. I have already argued that any such account is unacceptable as a story of liberal community. In other words, while the escape shape is too negative, the pilgrimage shape is too positive. In order to provide a plausible public vocabulary for the shared life of a modern liberal political community, we need to locate a different kind of narrative shape. We need a narrative the shape of which is both less negative than escape, but yet less positive than pilgrimage. In the next chapter, and by appeal to narratives of quest, I shall begin to explore whether it is possible to identify a stable point somewhere between the negativity of escape and the positivity of pilgrimage, a point at which we can finally locate our account of liberal community.

Summary

In this chapter, I have considered the merits of a conception of liberal community that is structured so as to render it continuous with an understanding of community reflected by the so-called 'spirit of the blitz'. I began with the image of such a community as a negative, 'object-centred' association – essentially an inverted version of the traditional communities structured around the pursuit of a common good which I considered in Chapter 3. This negative conception of community is structured around the shared resistance of common hazards. I proceeded to suggest that in this image of communal life it was possible to see reflected the narrative structure of an escape. Fellow escapees are united by their shared flight from a specific origin; theirs too is a negative object-centred relationship. And the escape narrative shape suggests a more abstract structure by which we might understand the shared life of a community as the shared resistance of common ills.

Next, I considered the question of whether the escape narrative shape could provide a plausible structure for the narrative of the shared life of the members of a liberal community. I appealed to Judith Shklar's 'liberalism of fear' in order to show that, in principle at least, it is possible to derive a conception of community from the escape narrative which is both realistically inclusive and able to provide a plausible account of the sense of belonging together which I have associated with the idea of a liberal community. However, I proceeded to argue that a community so conceived could provide only a partial interpretation of the shared life of a liberal polity. The problem is that liberal citizens are running for rather more than just their lives. The escape model implies that the shared life of a liberal community is exhausted by its search for minimal peace and security, but that is not true. The escape model fails to distinguish the sense in which the negative community is a negative *liberal* community.

This defect of the escape model leaves us, I suggested, in a rather awkward position. We need to supplement the escape shape with a rather less negative account of liberal community, but the only other account we have at our disposal at this stage is the discredited pilgrimage model. That model is no good because it accounts for liberal community only by appealing to an unacceptably exclusionary comprehensive conception of the liberal good. What is needed, then, is a narrative shape which will serve to differentiate a distinctively liberal community, but which does so without having to appeal to a comprehensive and controversial destination or purpose for the liberal society. The story of the liberal polity can certainly begin with escape, but it cannot end there. The story must go on, but it cannot go on as a pilgrimage. In the next chapter I shall explore the possibility that perhaps it might go on as a quest.

5

Community as Quest

> The word 'community' is much used in political philo-
> sophy. I think the true communities in modern life are
> to be found in professions and shared pursuits, in the
> communities of people who work together. Most lawyers,
> most actors, most soldiers and sailors, most athletes, most
> doctors, and most diplomats feel a certain solidarity in the
> face of outsiders, and, in spite of other differences, they
> share fragments of a common ethic in their working life,
> and a kind of moral complicity. (Hampshire, 1999, 49)

Here, Stuart Hampshire identifies an understanding of community
significantly different from those I have so far articulated. By a community of people who work together, I take it that Hampshire does
not have in mind, say, closely related business partners, those who
work together in order to achieve a clearly defined common goal.
Rather, he means to emphasize the bond between those who work
together in a somewhat looser sense, those who share a common
profession and a common professional morality. In other words,
Hampshire means to highlight the possibility of a community that
is not structured by its shared pursuit of a good. For example, professional politicians of opposing political parties do not share in the
pursuit of a common goal; they are not bound together by a
common object. But they are nevertheless bound together; their
relationship is expressed in their shared activity. As Hampshire
observes, 'through all their hostilities,' professional politicians may
still 'recognise their similarities of habit' (Hampshire, 1999, 49). 'It is

easy to underestimate the acute professional pleasure that politicians of sharply hostile purposes may take in their negotiations with each other and in the processes of manoeuvre and counter-manoeuvre. They recognise and respect in each other a passion and a pleasure, sometimes almost an addiction which they do not share with the unpolitical mass of mankind' (Hampshire, 1989, 176). Those who work together in this way, as fellow professionals, are united neither by their shared pursuit of a common good, nor (primarily at least) by their shared resistance of common ills. They do not share a common purpose; they share only a common process.

In this chapter I want to explore this model of community life and to consider whether or not it can provide a plausible interpretation of a liberal community. I shall replicate the formats of Chapters 3 and 4, and proceed in three stages. In the first section, and in order to get clearer about the form of the shared life suggested by the community of people who work together, I shall seek to develop an apparent structural resemblance between it and journey narratives of quest. In the second section, I shall consider the questions of whether and how the quest shape I have articulated can be applied at the level of the liberal state. In so doing, I shall explain how what I shall term 'procedural' accounts of liberal community, traces of which can be found in the work of Stuart Hampshire and also a number of other 'political' liberals and democratic procedural-ists, seem in certain important respects to reflect the quest shape. Finally, in the third section, I shall consider whether or not the quest model provides a plausible and appealing interpretation of the shared life of the members of a liberal society by examining how effectively it responds to the fundamental challenge I have set of showing how liberal community might be realized in a context of pluralism and conflict.

The quest narrative

The term 'quest' has been subjected to a great deal of use, misuse and general abuse over time. The term 'has been applied to narratives involving journeys of all sorts or no spatial journeys at all, as if the mere word were an explanation: this or that character is "on a quest" or "in quest of" something' (Stout, 1983, 87–8). But we need more precision here if we are to put the narrative to philosophical service. I want to use the term to denote a certain class of narratives including, for example, *The Quest of The Holy Grail*, Miguel de Cervantes's *Don Quixote*, and Jack Kerouac's *On The Road*. I do not mean to claim that the account of the term that I shall elaborate in this section is final and authoritative. I mean only to delineate the kind of narrative shape with which I shall be concerned in this chapter.

The central point I want to emphasize is that the quest designates a kind of narrative quite distinct from the pilgrimages and escapes I have discussed in the previous two chapters. Whereas the focus of the pilgrimage narrative is upon the destination, and the focus of the escape narrative is upon the origin, the quest narrative focuses our attention on the journey *itself*. The distinction between pilgrimage and quest is partly epistemological. Typically, pilgrims know where their journey ends. In *The Pilgrim's Progress*, Christian knew that his journey ended at the Celestial City. In *The Canterbury Tales*, the pilgrims knew that their journey ended in Canterbury. By contrast, questers are generally uncertain about their destination. This is neatly dramatized in *The Quest of The Holy Grail* when the author describes the departure of the knights of the round table, explaining how they struck 'out into the forest one here, one there, wherever they saw it thickest and wherever path or track was absent' (Matarasso (trans.), 1969, 52–3). Or, as Malory has it, 'every knight took the way that him liked best' (Malory, 1998, 320). Similarly, Cervantes reports the manner in which Don Quixote seeks to follow 'only the path his horse wished to take, believing that the virtue of his adventures lay in doing this' (Cervantes, 2005, 25). Kerouac's Sal Paradise is less equivocal about his journey across the United States with his companion, Dean Moriaty, stating plainly that 'I didn't know where all this was leading' (Kerouac, 1991, 112).

But in fact the distinction between the pilgrimage and the quest is sometimes far starker than this. It would be a mistake to think of questers as pilgrims in need of a map. It is not simply that they do not know where they are going; the fact of the matter is that the quest's geographical destination just isn't very important. Having explained that he 'didn't know where all this was leading', Sal adds that he 'didn't care' (Kerouac, 1991, 112). This is a reasonable thing for a quester to say because it is not necessarily the journey's destination that invests the quest with its meaning. Sal's journeys typically take him out West to Los Angeles, but it would be quite wrong to suggest that the *purpose* of his journey is to get to L.A.[1] The point is that in narratives of quest, the journey's destination and the journey's purpose tend to diverge. The journey's meaning seems chiefly to derive not from the destination, but from the process of travelling itself. The idea, or hope, is that some good will be realized in and through the journey quite independent of wherever it may happen to end up.

A further important, and distinctive, feature of the quest narrative is that, as Stout suggests, it is 'a journey of search, a pursuit of the unknown'. Most questers are sustained in their travails by the belief that the journey will reveal some 'radically significant' yet 'radically uncertain' good (Stout, 1983, 88). Consider the moment in *The Quest of the Holy Grail* at which the knights at Camelot are first presented with a vision of the Grail they will go on to seek:

> The Holy Grail appeared, covered with a cloth of white samite; and yet no mortal hand was seen to bear it. It entered through the great door, and at once the palace was filled with fragrance as though all the spices of the earth had been spilled abroad. It circled the hall along the great tables and each place was furnished in its wake with the food its occupants desired. When all were served, the Holy Grail vanished, they knew not how nor whither. (Matarasso, 1969, 44)

It is important to emphasize here that the Holy Grail is *covered*; the knights know that they are witnessing something sublime, but they do not really know what that thing is. Similarly, Sal Paradise is moved by the compulsive sense that his journey will yield some deeply uncertain yet highly important discovery, achievement or experience. Somewhere 'along the line I knew there'd be girls, visions, everything; somewhere along the line the pearl would be handed to me' (Kerouac, 1991, 10). MacIntyre notes that a quest is not at all 'a search for something already adequately characterized, as miners search for gold or geologists for oil. It is in the course of the quest and only through encountering and coping with the various particular harms, dangers, temptations and distractions which provide any quest with its episodes and incidents that the goal of the quest is finally to be understood' (MacIntyre, 1985, 219). The 'Grail', the 'Pearl', 'Justice', 'America': so many placeholders for great goods unknowable in advance of the search, great goods discoverable only in and through the shared process of seeking.

And it is the attraction of such goods that distinguishes journeys of quest from journeys of escape. Stout observes that escape and quest are often related, 'the difference arising from the question of which motivation is stronger, the repellent force or the attracting goal' (Stout, 1983, 99). The Knights of the Round Table are certainly repelled by the corruption of Camelot, but their journey is a quest and not an escape because the attraction of the Grail provides the stronger motivation. Sal Paradise reports that his departure involves 'leaving confusion and nonsense behind' (Kerouac, 1991, 121). If that were the whole story, then his journey would be one of escape. But as he explains, he is not only fleeing bewilderment; he is also 'performing the one and noble function of the time, *move*' in quest of the Pearl (Kerouac, 1991, 121). In other words, quests differ from escapes by virtue of their more positive preoccupations. Whereas the coherence and structure of the escape is given by the negativity of the repellent force, the coherence and structure of the quest is given by the journey and by the hope of the great good it may eventually disclose.

In summary, then, quests are journeys structured by and primarily focused upon the process of travelling itself, a process which it is thought will yield some great, though uncertain, good or discovery. Like an escape, the journey typically constitutes a movement away from something negative, but it differs from the escape in its more positive outlook: the value of the journey is not exhausted by the fact that it takes us away from the bad thing. However, and unlike journeys of pilgrimage, the value of the journey is not completed by the fact that it brings us closer to some predetermined destination. The quest remains an open-ended journey; its primary value resides in the journey itself and stands free from both origins and destinations.

The quest narrative suggests the possibility of a life possessing a shape quite different from those we have encountered so far. A life possessing the shape of a quest is a life without a strong sense of positive purpose, without a strong sense of what it is supposed to achieve, but with the conviction that a good may be realized by living in a certain way. Where one's life ends up is, on this view, not always as important as the way in which it is lived. In other words, a person living a quest-shaped life would be liable to associate a value with living in a certain way independent of considerations relating to where such a life might lead. Similarly, the quest suggests a shared life that congeals around a process rather than an outcome. It calls to mind a more 'nomadic' view of the shared life. To share in a life shaped like a quest is not to agree upon any particular goal. As Dean Moriaty puts it: 'What's your road, man? – holyboy road, madman road, rainbow road, guppy road, any road. It's an any-where road for anybody anyhow' (Kerouac, 1991, 229). The unity of those who share such a life is expressed not in their understand-ing of the end of the road, but in the road itself: the process of travelling together and searching for the Pearl.

We can now see the way in which the quest narrative is reflected in the communities of people who work together that I described at the beginning of the chapter. Professional politicians, an example of a shared profession that Hampshire emphasizes, are rarely united by their pursuit of a common goal or destination. They are in no substantial agreement about where they want their society to go, where they want their shared journey to end. Indeed, they may dis-agree very sharply indeed. Their unity is expressed instead in their shared commitment to the institutional processes to which they are subject: the process of travelling and the 'rules of the road'. Pro-fessional politicians of opposing viewpoints are united by their shared commitment to broadly democratic procedures and by their conviction that an important value attaches to shared democratic activity. Their shared life may be conceived as a quest for that value. I shall now consider the possibility that the shared life of the members of a liberal polity could be conceived as possessing the shape of a quest.

Liberal community as quest

I have suggested that narratives of quest imply a particular vision of the shared life and, hence, a particular vision of community. The quest model of community is the model of a *procedural* community, a community defined neither by the goods it pursues nor primarily by the ills it resists, but rather by the shared activities it involves.

This suggests an understanding of political community quite closely related to Michael Oakeshott's conception of 'civil association'. Civil associates are conceived as 'persons (*cives*) related to one another, not in terms of a substantive undertaking, but in the terms of the common acknowledgement of civil (not instrumental) laws specifying conditions to be subscribed to in making choices and in performing self-chosen actions' (Oakeshott, 1975, 313). Oakeshott suggests that the disposition to civil association may find its source in a disposition of human character 'to prefer the road to the inn, ambulatory conversation to deliberation about means for achieving ends, the rules of the road to directions about how to reach a destination' (Oakeshott, 1975, 324). Evidently, this is very much the character of the questing companions, like Sal Paradise and Dean Moriaty, whom I discussed in the last section. And I have suggested that we can see this kind of procedural, quest community realized in the communities of people who work together, people who 'share fragments of a common ethic in their working life, and a kind of moral complicity' in spite of their substantial moral differences. The question I want now to consider is whether this idea of procedural community could be replicated at the level of the liberal polity. Could the quest model provide a plausible interpretation of liberal political community?

It is something very much like this question that has animated the enquiries of those who have come to be known as 'political liberals'. Political liberals have, on one interpretation at least, sought to show that it is plausible to think of the citizens of a liberal society as constituting a community of people who work together. The central idea here is relatively straightforward and familiar. Liberal citizens, on this view, can readily pursue divergent goals and values without undermining the unity of their association, because the unity of their association is not carried in the goals they pursue; it is carried instead in their shared devotion to a liberal conception of justice; a shared procedural ethic. Commitment to the liberal conception of justice is compatible with pluralism and conflict because it stands relatively free from comprehensive conceptions of morality and the good life.

It is worth pausing here to clarify the attribution of 'freestandingness'. The key idea is that the liberal political conception is presented neither as being, nor as being derived from, a comprehensive moral, religious or philosophical doctrine (Rawls, 1996, 12). The attribution does not imply that the political conception presupposes no substantial moral claims whatsoever, it insists only that any substantial moral claims which are presupposed must be claims which can be freely acknowledged by all reasonable citizens. In other words, the procedure aims to be such as to provide the focus of an 'overlapping consensus'. And the point of 'the idea of an overlapping consensus on a political conception is to show how, despite a diversity of doctrines, convergence on a political conception of justice may be achieved and social unity sustained in long-run equilibrium' (Rawls, 1999, 426). In other words, the hope is that whatever other various, divergent and conflicting enterprises the members of a liberal society may pursue, they will all nevertheless be able to endorse certain terms of moral association.

This is the core idea, but still it requires some spelling out. The unity of the procedural, quest community is expressed, I have suggested, in citizens' shared identification with a liberal political conception of justice. Because this conception of justice is freestanding from comprehensive conceptions of morality and the good, it is possible to justify it to an otherwise divided citizenry. In this way, the requirement of justifiability that is central to liberal conceptions of community is potentially satisfied. However, this 'answer' to the problem of community rather seems to bring us back to where we first started. As I suggested in Chapter 1, mere justifiability is often thought insufficient to deliver the depth of community and integration that matters to many liberals. To achieve that depth of community, it is necessary for the liberal political conception to be *publicly* justifiable. Citizens must feel not only that they belong to the polity, but also that they belong together. The commitment to the liberal conception has to be grounded in a *common* point of view. I have already noted David Miller's argument that it would be a mistake to imagine that a shared commitment to just rules alone could provide an adequate basis for a community of the kind liberals typically seek:

> The kind of ties we are looking for are not external and mechanical, but involve each person seeing his life as part and parcel of the wider group, so that the question of how well his own life is going depends in some measure on how well the

community as a whole is faring. This brings in issues of common good, historical identity, and so forth which reach far beyond the scope of distributive justice. Rawls's notion that adherence to a shared conception of distributive justice could form a sufficient basis for community is quite implausible (Miller, 1989, 60).

The suspicion, then, is that justifiability alone will not provide a sufficient basis for liberal community. As Galston writes, the 'liberal state cannot be understood along Michael Oakeshott's lines as a purposeless civil association structured by adverbial rules. Like every other form of political community, the liberal state is an enterprise association. Its distinctiveness lies not in the absence but, rather, in the content of its public purposes' (Galston, 1991, 3). The procedural community can only flourish if the shared commitment to the liberal political conception is grounded in a common point of view such as that provided by a shared identity. In other words, it is thought that in order to provide a satisfactory basis for community, the commitment to liberal justice must reflect a deeper commonality, a commonality that is going to be very hard to reconcile with the reasonable pluralism of a liberal society. For, otherwise, the members of the liberal society cannot be expected to experience themselves as bound to respond to the requirements of the liberal political conception. In short, the procedural conception of community was the *problem* from which my discussion began; it cannot now be ushered back in as the *solution*. Conceived in such purely procedural terms, the quest community is no community at all.

But here it looks as though the quest narrative may be of some assistance. It is clear that questing companions do share more than an 'external and mechanical' commitment to the rules of the road. The rules provide a framework for the shared journey, but they do not explain it. Questing companions share a commitment to their journey because they believe that in and through it they may realize a great good: the Pearl or the Grail. Returning, then, to the quest model of community, we might say that it is not grounded solely in a shared commitment to liberal justice. Rather, it is grounded in a shared commitment to liberal justice *which is itself grounded* in the idea that we share with our fellow citizens in the search for a good. The members of such an association endorse the liberal conception of justice because they believe that it constitutes an expression of their deeper commonality as fellow searchers for the Grail.

At first sight, this may seem to be of no help at all. It is not open to us to suppose that the shared commitment to the liberal process is explained by the way in which such commitment expresses a shared conception of the good, because a shared conception of the good is precisely what liberal citizens must necessarily lack. That is exactly why the likes of Miller have thought it necessary to cultivate commonality in the form of a shared, largely invented and inculcated, national identity. But this worry overlooks the point I stressed in the previous section that the Pearl and the Grail are just 'placeholders' for a good that is antecedently unknowable. Recall MacIntyre's observation that it 'is in the course of the quest and only through encountering and coping with the various particular harms, dangers, temptations and distractions which provide any quest with its episodes and incidents that the goal of the quest is finally to be understood' (MacIntyre, 1985, 219). As Jeffrey Stout explains, MacIntyre's characterization of the quest denies that the good is 'something we first know, capture in theory and then pursue' (Stout, 2001, 238). That, of course, is the view of the comprehensive liberals like Galston who defend a conception of community conforming to the pilgrimage model I set out in Chapter 3. Galston provides in advance an account of the flourishing liberal community which good liberal citizens are then expected to pursue.

But the quest model is different. It is far more 'open-ended' than the pilgrimage model. In advance of the quest we can specify only a 'provisional' conception of the good which may very well be envisaged differently by different companions. All companions suppose that their shared journey may realize a great good, but how each conceives of that good may well be different, and such disagreement need not be undermining of the fellowship between them. For example, there is no doubt that Gawain and Galahad differ in their provisional conceptions of the Grail: Gawain supposes that the quest is directed purely towards the realization of the courtly ideal (courage, magnanimity, courtesy and *savoir-faire*), completely overlooking any spiritual dimension, whereas for Galahad the sacred dimension of the enterprise is central (Matarasso, 1969, 19). Even so, they still regard one another, at the outset at least, as companions in the quest, and this is because they conceive of themselves as sharing in the pursuit of the Grail.

Consequently, to say that questing companions are united by their shared pursuit of the Pearl or the Grail is not at all to say that they share a comprehensive conception of the good life; it is rather to say that they share a commitment to the pursuit of an antecedently unknowable, provisional good. As Stout writes:

> If we think of our society as oriented, by virtue of shared inten-
> tions and a self-limiting consensus on the good, toward a provi-
> sional *telos*, we should be able to avoid thinking of the question,
> 'individual freedom or common purpose?' as presenting an exclu-
> sive choice. We have so little sense of common purpose in part
> because we have become so accustomed to a picture that hides
> the actual extent of our commonality from view. We need also to
> remember that preserving a healthy degree of individual freedom
> inheres in our common purpose and helps define our conception
> of justice. (Stout, 2001, 237)

In other words, we share with our fellow citizens not a fully articu-lated and comprehensive conception of the good life, but rather the belief that there *is* a good to be known in common that cannot be known alone. Fellow citizens are, in Dworkin's sense, 'integrated'; they may differ as to what they think it means to 'win' or to 'lose', but they nevertheless 'know that they win or lose together' (Dworkin, 2000, 234). This interpretation of the quest model seems to suggest that it is possible for the shared commitment to liberal justice displayed by the members of a procedural liberal community to be grounded in a deeper commonality (and hence satisfy the requirement of public justifiability) notwithstanding the reasonable pluralism of the liberal society. This is because the deeper common-ality in which the shared commitment to the liberal process is grounded is a provisional commonality: our shared commitment to the Grail.

There is a very important ambiguity in the formulation I have offered here of the Grail as a good to be known in common that cannot be known alone. I indicated the ambiguity in the previous section, but I it may be helpful now to bring it right out into the open. It is unclear whether the (uncertain) good of the quest is something 'out there', something to be found rather as Galahad and his companions find the Grail, or whether the good is simply the (uncertain) good of searching itself – a truly procedural good. On the former interpretation, the distinction between the Grail-quest and the pilgrimage is essentially epistemological. Pilgrims know where they are going and what they expect to find, questers do not. On the latter interpretation, there is a more dramatic difference between the two kinds of narrative. If the good of the quest consists in the searching, then the meaningfulness of the journey resides not at the journey's end, but on the journey itself. It seems to me that this ambiguity is characteristic of many quest narratives. In this chapter, I suppose something like the former: the Holy Grail is a unitary, though uncertain good, to be attained through the quest. However, I shall return to this ambiguity in the next chapter, and shall suggest that perhaps the latter interpretation – that the good in common is realized in the journey itself – is a more promising way of thinking about the quest model of political community.

For the time being, the view we are considering is that the quest model, and specifically the idea of the provisional good it reveals, provides an account of how a procedural liberal community might satisfy the rather stringent requirement of public justifiability in a context of moral conflict. Members of a procedural liberal community (conceived as conforming to the quest model) experience themselves as bound to obey the demands of the liberal polity on the grounds that their obedience contributes to the attainment of the provisional good – a good in common that cannot be known alone.

This model provides us with a quite distinctive image of communal life. The procedural community is not an association of persons striving to realize an ideal antecedently specified and endorsed like Galston's account of the liberal good. Nor is it merely an association of persons striving to resist a handful of common ills. It suggests rather an association of persons striving together, working together to know a good. This is a vision of community which bears some relation to the view of democratic community articulated by Carol Gould:

> The idea of democracy, in itself, ... presupposes community in a minimal sense, namely, that people in a democratically operating

institution have a common interest in shared ends, in pursuit of which their cooperation is voluntary and not merely constrained by law or habit or effected by coercion. Such a community is constituted by the decisions of agents to engage in the determination of these ends and by free cooperation toward attaining them. (Gould, 2004, 46)

Like the quest model, Gould locates community not in an antecedently specified shared end, but in the pursuit and determination of a shared end.

However, part of my concern here has been to resist, or at least clarify, the suggestion, which Gould makes, that such a community must be regarded as 'minimal'. There is a sense in which the account certainly is minimal. The quest model of liberal community is a model of a shared *political* life and there is no suggestion here that a shared political life should be equated with a shared life as a whole. In this connection, Dworkin offers the illuminating example of an orchestra:

The communal life of an orchestra is limited to producing orchestral music: it is *only* a musical life. ... The musicians treat their performances together as the performance of their orchestra personified, and they share in its triumphs and failures as their own. But they do not suppose that the orchestra also has a sex life, in some way composed of the sexual activities of its members, or that it has headaches, or high blood pressure, or responsibilities of friendship, or crises over whether it should care less about music and take up photography instead. (Dworkin, 2000, 227)

We may similarly insist that the shared life of the quest model of liberal political community is limited to politics: it is *only* a political life. Thus, it might be said that the 'scope' of the liberal community is limited or minimal, but there need be nothing minimal about the depth of integration or belonging in the community. We might think that the intensity of one's attachment to the liberal community would inevitably have to be limited due to the lack of comprehensive commonality between liberal citizens, but I have suggested that the device of the Grail, the provisional good, allows the possibility that this sort of community could be expressive of deep commonality and belonging without the kind of comprehensive moral consensus which many have taken to be necessary for a meaningful form of community.

In summary, then, I have argued that the quest narrative suggests an image of the shared life of a liberal polity which manages to be both distinctively liberal and yet open-ended. The quest model is distinctively liberal because it conceives of the shared life of a liberal polity as structured by a liberal process. And it is open-ended because a procedural ethic is all it is: it does not specify in advance exactly what we are working towards. The social unity of such an association is not expressed in a conception of the good shared by all members, but in their shared belief that there is a good to be known in common that cannot be known alone.

In this way, it seems that we may finally have located an accurate and appealing account of the shared life of a liberal political community. The suggestion is that we think of the life of a liberal polity as a life of escape which, in good times at least, merges into quest. In other words, our unity is expressed, first and foremost, in our recognition of our common vulnerabilities and in our shared resistance to the ills that afflict us all. However, when times are good, and when politics goes well, our unity is expressed in another, and rather less negative, way. It is expressed in our shared devotion to a liberal political process which itself reflects our belief that a great, though uncertain, good is to be achieved through a certain (liberal) way of living together. I shall now begin to consider whether this is an adequate account. Does the quest model really provide a satisfactory interpretation of the liberal political community?

Assessing the quest model

As I have indicated, the quest model appears, on the surface at least, to be very promising. On the theoretical plane, it suggests the possibility of a meaningful form of distinctively liberal community which is nevertheless compatible with the reasonable pluralism of a liberal society. It is inclusive of moral diversity and conflict and yet potentially constitutes an object of robust enthusiasm for citizens who conceive of their provisional good as intimately bound up in the life of the association. On the practical plane, it seems to provide a phenomenologically plausible account of the practices of trust, concern and belonging that I identified in the Introduction. I argued in the previous chapter that those practices are readily traceable to our shared recognition of a common vulnerability. Now we might add that the quest model can plausibly account for the less negative attraction that many of us have to the life we share with those around us. Many of us feel that the value of our shared life is not exhausted by its concern to resist the things we deem to be evil. The device of the provisional good or Grail central to the quest model explains how it is not unreasonable to feel this way notwithstanding the sharp moral disagreements that mark our societies.

But superficial appearances may be deceiving. It seems to me that there is a rather serious problem here which can be brought out by appeal, once again, to the quest narrative. As I stressed earlier, quest-ing companions, unlike pilgrims and escapees, do not really care about what exactly lies at the road's end or beginning – the mean-ingfulness of the quest does not derive from either its destination or its origin. Instead, it generally derives from the belief that some great, though mysterious, good may be discovered by travelling together in a certain way: the Grail, the pearl and so on. In other words, the meaning of the quest and its coherence as a journey seem to depend crucially on the faith of its participants that there is, indeed, a good out there to be found. Herein lies the problem: should the parties to the quest lose their faith in the Grail or the pearl, then nothing will remain to structure the journey or to invest it with meaning. If the parties to the quest lose their faith in the Grail, they are lost.

It is striking that, in *The Quest of the Holy Grail*, the question of being lost never arises. Certainly, most of the questing knights fail in their search for the Grail, but there is never any serious question of the Grail's not being out there to be discovered by a suitably virtuous knight, like Galahad. The reason for this is straightforward; the knights of the Grail-fellowship know that the Grail is certainly out there to be found, because they know that God put it there. The inhabitants of an enchanted world invested with meaning by the hand of a supernatural power can rest assured that there is indeed a great good out there somewhere to be found. But times have changed and the tone of the modern quest has darkened. As Janis Stout writes:

> In a disheartened and disheartening social atmosphere, a society of anomie, uncertainty and scepticism, the questing hero may find not only that he cannot reach transcendently noble goals but also that he cannot formulate goals at all or that he loses sight of those he has formulated. When this occurs, the quest ... becomes absorbed into the pattern, or nonpattern, of the journey of wandering, the journey of the lost hero. (Stout, 1983, 101)

This seems ultimately to be the fate of Sal Paradise in *On The Road*. His early exuberance – the whole country was 'like an oyster for us to open; and the pearl was there, the pearl was there' (Kerouac, 1991, 124) – is balanced by a nagging sense of futility, the suspicion that he is simply lost: 'Gad, what was I doing three thousand miles from home? Why had I come here?' No answer is provided (Kerouac, 1991, 68). This gradual loss of faith in the journey and the pearl it was supposed to reveal reaches its culmination at the novel's end which finds Sal reviling 'the senseless nightmare road. All of it inside endless and beginningless emptiness' (Kerouac, 1991, 231). The overwhelming sense is one of being trapped, frantically 'zigzagging between arbitrary terminal points on linear reaches into emptiness' (Stout, 1983, 110).

And it seems to me that a similar sense of futility must necessarily pervade the quest model of liberal community as I have so far characterized it. The structure and meaning of the procedural community derives not from the evils it resists, nor the comprehensive goods it pursues, but from the faith expressed in Michael Sandel's insistence that 'when politics goes well we can know a good in common that we cannot know alone' (Sandel, 1982, 183). Unfortunately, politics very rarely goes well. In the conditions of modernity, it is going to be very difficult if not impossible to sustain the belief that our shared political life holds out the promise of any sort of common good at all. This 'conception of a political order, as a social union which enables individuals to know a good in common that they cannot know alone, expresses a wish for a degree of social unity which is simply inconsistent with the extent of diversity, mobility, and disagreement in the modern world' (Kukathas,

2003, 258). For us, there is no Holy Grail waiting just beyond the horizon. Procedural community is an expression of wishful thinking, a consoling delusion of the lost. John Updike's Reverend Eccles puts it very neatly: 'Of course, all vagrants think they're on a quest. At least at first.' (Updike, 1961, 128).

The objection here can be put more formally. I appealed to the device of the Holy Grail as a way of rendering the procedural community a positive yet non-comprehensive enterprise. The shared life of such a community is characterized not by the shared pursuit of a clearly defined and comprehensive goal, as was the case in the pilgrimage model, but rather by the shared pursuit of a provisional good, the substance of which is unknowable in advance. This seems to provide a distinctive grounding for social unity in conditions of moral conflict. For example, the economic conservative and the progressive may very well have sharply divergent views about the substance of the common good in the pursuit of which they share, but the hope is that they might nevertheless agree that they share in the pursuit of a common good of some sort. But now I have put that hope to the question. Can we really expect conservatives and progressives to believe that their political life is directed towards the realization of a common good?

Are we to believe that the professional politicians with whom I began this chapter really believe that in spite of all of their moral differences they are going to be able to discover a good in common they could not have known alone? To be sure, Gould's view of democratic community might continue to hold. Professional politicians might well conceive of themselves as sharing in the determination of a shared end. But it seems far more plausible to interpret this kind of common activity as the shared determination of a rather messy compromise than as the shared determination of a common good. The picture of the shared life of the modern liberal society as a quest for the common good is extremely difficult to sustain in the face of moral pluralism and the interminable conflicts it seems to engender. Of course one might, like Jeffrey Stout, stress here the moral beliefs we do share (Stout, 2001, 237; Chapter 1); it would certainly be a distortion to claim that we moderns exhibit no moral consensus whatsoever. But I do not think that such a response really meets the objection being levelled here. The claim is not, or not only, that we do not have enough in common to be able plausibly to conceive of ourselves as sharing in the pursuit of an as yet unknown good in common; the claim is that it is far from clear why we should regard substantial moral and political convergence as an appropriate political aspiration in the first place. Without the supernatural assurance of the possibility of a final harmony enjoyed by the knights of the grail-quest, the inclination to strive for moral convergence can actually begin to seem rather peculiar.

It seems to me that a more natural reading of the political reality is that presented by the political liberals. Hampshire puts the point this way:

> The distinction of humanity, and its interest in its own eyes, lies in the variety and unending competition of ideals and languages, and in the absurdity of a moral Esperanto. ... The clash of moral and religious loyalties has come to seem, in the light of recent history, much more than a temporary accident of human development, to be dispelled by the spreading natural sciences and by healthy enlightenment. Rather the deep-seated spiritual antagonisms have come to seem the essence of humanity, and it is an accident of history if, in some regions and for some period of time, a relative harmony of shared values prevails within a modern society. (Hampshire, 1993, 43)

Pluralism, as Rawls has it, is 'a permanent feature of the public culture of democracy' (Rawls, 1996, 36). There is no reason to expect moral convergence and, for at least some political liberals, there is no reason even to desire it. From this point of view, the characterization of the shared life of a liberal society as a quest, as a striving for convergence, can be nothing other than a perverse distortion of the political reality, a stubborn and naïve resistance to the evidence of history and experience.

The Holy Grail presents a theoretically plausible method of reconciling a positive view of the shared life of a liberal polity with pronounced pluralism, but its representation of the shared life of the polity as life shaped by the striving for moral convergence is so radically at odds with the political liberal interpretation of the normal tendencies of broadly liberal democratic societies as to render it entirely implausible as an account of liberal political community. But if we lose faith in the Grail, if we lose faith in either the possibility or the desirability of convergence, then it seems that there is nothing left to hold us together as a liberal community, nothing at least beyond the external and mechanical, non-publicly justified commitment to the rules that Miller rejected; it seems that we have exhausted all other alternatives. The dark fear, I suppose, is that in the final analysis this must be true. As a collective we are necessarily lost, lost in the performance of a pointless and random ritual, tilting at windmills with a cohort of questionable strangers. What if the road is open only to a community of beatniks, bohemians and other deluded vagrants: the crazed Don Quixotes of our age?

Conclusion: The spectre of Don Quixote

It seems to me that the spectre of Don Quixote looms large over contemporary discussions of liberal political community. As I argued in the Introduction, it is possible to identify a bond between the citizens of actually existing liberal democratic societies. We are not simply strangers to one another. Many of us are inclined to identify ourselves to some extent with the broadly liberal institutions to which we are subject: we display attitudes of trust and mutual concern towards our fellow citizens and we also have some sense of integration in the common political life of the polity. In other words, we do not look entirely unlike a liberal moral community. But I have struggled to capture this bond in theory. It is not, I have suggested, plausibly captured by appeal to a shared comprehensive ideal, such as that provided by a shared conception of the liberal good. Nor, in any case, does the pilgrimage model provide in theory a satisfactorily liberal account of community. I have suggested that the bond is more plausibly captured by appeal to our common vulnerabilities and a shared conception of great evils. But, I have argued that such an account of the shared life – the escape model – is indeterminate. It does not, of itself, distinguish a liberal community. Consequently, the escape model is incomplete until something has been said about its positive face.

This conclusion prompted the move I have made in this chapter to the quest narrative and the procedural view of community. While this account seems to provide an accurate interpretation of political community which is also congenial to liberals, it seems too 'thin' to motivate consistent obedience and the kinds of attitudes we would normally associate with the idea of a liberal community. Stout's strategy for 'thickening' the kind of commitment involved in the procedural community by appeal to the device of the Holy Grail or provisional good constituted a theoretically coherent response. However, it is a response that is rendered implausible by the facts of history and experience, which offer no reason for the members of a modern society to anticipate substantial moral convergence. And yet, in spite of all of this, the members of liberal societies normally identify themselves with the institutions to which they are subject and display attitudes of trust, concern and belonging towards their fellow citizens. The problem is that, without a theory to account for this behaviour, they seem as delusional as Don Quixote.

The puzzle here is perhaps most neatly set not by Cervantes's Don Quixote, but by Graham Greene's Sancho in his pastiche, *Monsignor Quixote*. Greene's novel tells of the journey undertaken by the Roman Catholic, Father Quixote, and his friend, the deposed communist mayor, Zancas (or 'Sancho', as Father Quixote affection-ately refers to him). The journey has no obvious purpose beyond Sancho's concern that Father Quixote buys some socks, and the two men are clearly troubled by their lack of commonality. Father Quixote says, 'I doubt very much whether we are the right compan-ions, you and I. A big gulf separates us, Sancho' (Greene, 2000, 37). And, then, at the point of their departure, Sancho sets what I take to be a fundamental puzzle:

> 'We must have something in common, father, or why do you go with me?' (Greene, 2000, 44)

Both men are aware that they have little or nothing in common: they recognize and pursue different conceptions of the good life and disagree profoundly with one another on moral and political matters. And yet they go together as companions on a journey. The puzzle is that, with nothing in common to hold them together and to render their unity intelligible, we are left unclear as to why Monsignor Quixote and Sancho should share with one another in a journey at all. Ought we to judge them as their ancestors were judged, as either simple-minded or mad?

I think this puzzle is central, and that its import extends far beyond Greene's preoccupations and the pages of his novel. It is a puzzle for us as well, a puzzle cast in particularly stark relief by the quest model of community. As Kukathas has written, many have recognized that 'it is the understandings people share that make them into a community' (Kukathas, 2003, 170). However, the pluralistic conditions of modernity dictate that the shared life of liberal citizens, if they are to have one at all, cannot be explained by appeal to a shared conception of the liberal good, regardless of whether that good is comprehensive or merely provisional. Consequently, it is unclear that the citizens of the liberal polity so conceived do in fact share any understandings at all (beyond, we may suppose, their commitment to the liberal process). And so, Sancho's question recurs: we must have something in common with our fellow citizens or why do we identify ourselves with one another and with the liberal political process? Can there be such a thing as a shared political life without a goal, a purposeless yet meaningful community? I conclude the discussion here with many more questions than answers, but there is yet hope. In Greene's novel, Father Quixote offers an answer to Sancho's question. In the next chapter, I shall examine that answer and argue that it provides the beginning of an entirely different understanding of the shared political life, one which holds out the prospect of a meaningful community of liberal citizens in conditions of moral and political conflict.

6

On Companionship

In many ways, the quest model of political community looks like the right sort of account for a morally divided liberal society. It is open-ended (unlike the pilgrimage model), so it allows for 'the open possibility of the invention of new and unforeseeable ways of life' (Hampshire, 1983, 28). Moreover, it can be distinctively liberal (unlike the escape model), for it focuses community on the shared commitment to a set of political rules and procedures. Of course these procedures do not have to be liberal, but they *can* be. In a sense, then, the quest model sets it sights higher than the mere safety and security sought by the members of a negative community; it insists that those within the community must adhere to a specifically liberal procedure.

Unfortunately, the procedural account, by itself, seems too thin to motivate a genuine sense of solidarity among its participants. An external and mechanical commitment to the rules is inadequate to ground a secure sense of community. What is needed is the deeper commonality provided by a shared identity. In the previous chapter, I suggested that perhaps the quest narrative shape might be of some assistance to us here. The device of the Holy Grail, understood as the placeholder for a great good unknowable in advance of the shared life, suggested the possibility that the members of the procedural community might be able to conceive of themselves as sharing in the pursuit of a good without actually agreeing on what that good consisted in. Ultimately, however, the quest model, so understood, was found wanting as an account of a political community in conditions of conflict. By presuming moral convergence to

be the appropriate ambition of the political community, it contradicted my premiss that pluralism about the good is permanent. If
we begin from the assumption that there will be no convergence on
the good, we cannot plausibly endorse a view of community the
coherence of which depends on the assumption that there could be
convergence on the good.

All of this seems to support the view from which I began this
study: conflict is undermining of community; a distinctively liberal
political community cannot flourish in conditions of conflict about
the good life. On the contrary, 'it is the understandings people share
that make them into a community' (Kukathas, 2003, 170). Political
liberalism is a theoretical position which holds that the only shared
understanding we can legitimately expect (and enforce) is a shared
understanding about justice or political procedure. If that is not
enough commonality for political community – and I have agreed
with the likes of Miller, Tamir and Kymlicka that it is not – then it
seems that political liberalism must indeed abandon the hope of
community and the stability it promises to provide. As a political
collective, we are lost. The awkwardness, I suggested, is nicely
expressed in a question posed by Graham Greene's Sancho: we must
have something in common, or why do you go with me?

But hope may yet lie in Monsignor Quixote's response to Sancho's
question. The response is interesting, because it gestures towards an
account of social unity quite unlike anything we have encountered
so far. Father Quixote does not, for instance, suggest that in spite of
all of their differences, they nevertheless agree that freedom is a
great good in the pursuit of which they can share. Nor does he
suggest that in spite of all of their differences, they nevertheless
agree that cruelty is a great evil in the resistance of which they can
share. Nor even does he suggest that in spite of all of their differences, they nevertheless agree that their journey might yield a great
good in common that they could not have known alone. In fact, he
does not appeal to agreement at all. What he says is this:

'I suppose – friendship?' (Greene, 2000, 44)

The tentativeness of Father Quixote's response is interesting here: he
responds not with an answer, but another question. The implication
is that all other explanations have been exhausted and that friend-

ship, however implausible it may seem, is the only thing that remains: the two men have nothing in common with each other but their friendship, and it is their friendship, therefore, which they must hope will hold them together and lend meaning to their journey. A further supposition, then, is that friendship is a bond potentially capable of uniting those who have nothing else in common with each other.

I wonder if Monsignor Quixote's response might help us out of our current impasse. Could the bond of friendship provide the basis for a liberal community capable of flourishing in conditions of conflict? I believe that it can and in this chapter and the next I shall try to defend that belief. While the idea of friendship as a political concept has been largely neglected in Anglo-American political philosophy, enjoying nothing like the attention it received in the classical era, there has in recent years been something of a resurgence of interest in the concept. However, it seems to me that it is only rarely that these treatments of the idea fully register the significance and magnitude of what they are suggesting: the shift to a view of political community as grounded in friendship is a radical shift which involves a fundamental transformation of the way in which we think about social unity and casts doubt on the approach to the puzzle of political community favoured by many liberal political philosophers.

In this chapter, I shall explain why I think the move to friendship involves a dramatic shift of perspective and also why it seems to me to provide the most promising basis for a liberal community capable of surviving in conditions of moral and political conflict. I shall approach this task by examining the different ways in which we might think about the nature of companionship. The chapter is divided into four sections. In the first, I shall set out three different ways of thinking about the nature of companionship (companions as consumers, as citizens and as friends) and will explain how the view of companionship as friendship constitutes a perspective quite different from the view I have favoured to this point. Sections 2, 3 and 4 are devoted to the further elaboration of the idea of companionship as friendship. In the second, I explain how the nature of friendship as a basic form of care and concern could be extended into an account of community capable of flourishing in conditions of conflict. In the third, I examine the way in which this account affects the way we think about the journey narratives that have occupied much of this study and particularly the way in which we think about the quest narrative. In the fourth section, I try to locate the view of community as friendship within the broader literature on political community and explain how it may offer a more fruitful approach than that which currently predominates.

Three paradigms

There are three quite fundamentally different ways of thinking about social unity. The first of these I shall term the 'consumer paradigm', the second I shall term the 'citizenship paradigm', the third I shall term the 'friendship paradigm'.[1] My use of the word 'paradigm' might be thought rather extravagant, but I stand by it because I do mean to suggest that there are some very big differences involved here. And it is important to stress that these paradigms are not intended to mark out three further models of communal life, to be added to the three – pilgrimage, escape and quest – that I have already articulated. Rather, I mean to suggest that these paradigms provide us with three different ways of understanding the character of the companionship that we can identify in each of the three journey shapes (and, indeed, in any other journey shape one might care to mention). The different journey shapes I have considered suggest different ways in which we might think about the *ends or the purposes* of journeys (or of communal associations); the models of companionship that I shall consider now suggest different ways in which we might think about the *relationship between travellers* (or members of the community). In this section, I want to explain what each of the different paradigms tells us about companionship and how it bears on the task at hand.

The consumer paradigm

As Martin Hollis suggests, the consumer paradigm presupposes 'that the basic political relation among us is contractual and that the political community factors as an association of private individuals whose public contributions are instrumental' (Hollis, 1996a, 153). This provides us with a strategic interpretation of companionship which can be applied to each of the three journey models we have so far encountered. In the case of the pilgrimage model of community, the idea is that there is a good I desire which I can access only by cooperating with my fellow citizens. Consequently, I sign up to a shared life with my fellow citizens because it serves my interests to do so. On this view, political community is founded on a mutual coincidence of wants; it is a cooperative venture for mutual advantage. Similarly, in the case of the escape model of community the idea is that I am confronted by a threat to myself that I can resist only by cooperating with my fellow citizens. Consequently, I sign up to a shared life with my fellow citizens because I will be at risk if I do not. Here, then, political community is founded on a mutual coincidence of vulnerabilities; it is a cooperative venture for mutual protection. Finally, in the case of the quest model of community the idea is that some good for me is attainable in and through a life shared with my fellow citizens. I sign up to the shared life of the community because I believe that my interests could be served by so doing, although in this case I am not altogether clear precisely how they will be so served. Like the pilgrimage model, political community here is founded on a mutual coincidence of wants; it is a co-operative venture for mutual advantage. The difference is that the advantage in question is unknowable in advance. I suppose the thought here is that one signs up to such a community because one predicts that on balance one's interests will be better served by so doing than if one were to 'go it alone'.

I do not intend to be detained long by the consumer paradigm, for it provides a view of association which I rejected at the very outset from the discussion of community as a matter of definitional fiat. The consumer paradigm renders the political community, whatever shape it may take, a strategic association, and in Chapter 1, I simply stipulated that, whatever else it may be, a community is a non-strategic (moral) association. I characterized strategic associations as mere *modi vivendi*, to be contrasted with community, and my stipulation was not purely arbitrary: there are reasons to resist the suggestion that strategic associations can plausibly be regarded as communities. The most obvious problems here are those of compliance and stability. If my commitment to the shared life of the polity is entirely instrumental, I am left no reason to stand by my fellow citizens when the chips are down for them but up for me. Similarly, if I were to feel that my advantage would be better served out of the community than in, I would have no reason to stay and every reason to go. One might want to insist that such associations for mutual advantage are nevertheless rightly regarded as communities, but it is impossible to deny that their character is markedly different from the integrated moral associations I have been concerned with in this study. In any the case, the consumer paradigm does not capture the concern of the vast majority of those liberals sympathetic to the idea of political community and so I shall dwell on it no longer.

The citizenship paradigm

The citizenship paradigm, by contrast, does seem to capture the concerns of those sympathetic to the idea of community. Indeed, it is by far the most prevalent view in the literature and it has informed my approach to the question of companionship in the previous three chapters. On this view, companionship is conceived non-strategically. Fellow citizens are bound together by their sense of shared identity or, as Hollis puts it, '*conscience collective*, a shared sense of morally binding incorporation in a collective undertaking' (Hollis, 1996a, 161). Because I regard myself as morally integrated in the collective undertaking, it is no longer morally open to me to withhold my support for the collective, even when so doing is to my personal advantage. On the citizenship paradigm I have other reasons, moral reasons, to display solidarity through thick and thin. On this view, we come together with our fellow citizens not because it is for our advantage to do so (though it may be), but because we recognize a 'deep reason' why we should associate together, like a shared conception of the good, a shared national identity or a shared religion. This view of companionship seems to fit rather more neatly with our intuitions about community and with the general tenor of the literature.

But, as it stands, there is some haziness here. Hollis notes that 'the abstract terms of incorporation are pretty indefinite, leaving it unclear quite who is to be deemed incorporated and quite what is the unifying bond' (Hollis, 1996a, 161). To say that companionship consists in the sense of shared identity is extremely vague. We might wonder where this shared identity is supposed to come from (see Kymlicka, 1996, 188). What exactly is the character of the collective undertaking in which we are incorporated? What is our 'deep reason' for associating with our fellow citizens? While it would be impossible, at this level of abstraction, to say very much about the content of the undertaking which informs the shared identity of citizen-companions, I have argued that we can say something about the 'shape' of the undertaking. And, in the last three chapters, I have provided three different accounts of the shape of a shared life, the shape of the collective undertaking. The pilgrimage narrative provides one possibility: I regard myself as morally integrated in the collective undertaking because I share with my fellow citizens in the belief that our enterprise will yield a great and common good. We have the shared identity of fellow pilgrims, of companions travelling to a common destination. The escape narrative provides another possibility: here I regard myself as morally integrated in the collective undertaking because I share with my fellow citizens in the belief that our enterprise will serve to resist a great and common evil. In this case we have the shared identity of fellow escapees, of companions fleeing a common threat. The quest narrative provides a third possibility: I regard myself as morally integrated in the collective undertaking because I share with my fellows in the belief that our enterprise will allow us to realize a good in common that we cannot know alone. We have the shared identity of companions in quest of the Grail.

The citizenship paradigm promises to overcome the problems of compliance I identified in the consumer paradigm, but as we have seen in the last three chapters, it is not unproblematic. The key difficulty is that it is vulnerable to pluralism. The citizenship paradigm endorses Kukathas's declaration that it is the (moral) understandings we share that make us into a community; consequently, it struggles when confronted with moral diversity. On the pilgrimage model, for example, community is conditional on our sharing an understanding of the goal of our collective undertaking. That is fine (or relatively so) if we form a religious community, like the Amish, who share a comprehensive conception of the good life; it is more troubling if we are the citizens of a modern democratic society who disagree quite profoundly about the good. In Chapter 3 I suggested that the move, favoured by the likes of Galston, to a parsimonious liberal conception of the good could help here, but the uneasiness persists. From the perspective of the citizenship paradigm, the pilgrimage model of the shared life does not deal well with diversity. The escape model fares better simply because it requires less agreement. A shared understanding with respect to the bad seems easier to secure than agreement on the good. However, the escape model provides an incomplete account of a distinctively liberal community because it requires no commitment to liberal principles or procedures. The quest model provides a possible candidate for the positive face of the escape, but the device of the Holy Grail upon which it seems to rely once again seems inhospitable to pluralism. The coherence of the model is conditional on the ability of citizens to believe that they might find a good in common with their companions that they could not have known alone. But the faith that there is a common good out there just waiting to be discovered is very hard to sustain amidst the diversity and conflict of a modern democratic society.

Consequently, a 'plural community' 'threatens to be a contradiction in terms, with "community" demanding that all members subscribe to a single shared identity and "plural" refusing this demand' (Hollis, 1996a, 163–4). Or, as Sancho has it, 'we must have something in common, father, or why do you go with me?' If community is conditional on moral consensus, then, in a society marked by pronounced moral conflict, it seems unattainable in anything but its most attenuated form. But now it is time to take a closer look at Monsignor Quixote's response to his companion. Could Kukathas be mistaken to insist that it is the understandings we share that make us into a community?

The friendship paradigm

In essence, the friendship paradigm is more straightforward than either the consumer or citizenship accounts of companionship. The friendship paradigm suggests that we participate in a collective undertaking with those with whom we share the liberal polity not primarily because we imagine that our interests are served by so doing, nor because we endorse the (moral) purposes of the undertaking, but simply because we care about each other, because we regard our companions in the undertaking as our friends. As Hollis explains, friendships in this context are to be understood as 'basic non-contractual relationships, which express the self rather than serve it' (Hollis, 1996a, 164). Presumably this is Monsignor Quixote's thought. He does not share the journey with Sancho because he supposes that it is to his advantage to do so, nor because he shares with him an understanding of the purpose of the journey; they share the journey quite simply because they are friends, and friendship here is conceived as 'basic' such that we could not appeal to anything further to explain its existence.

My appeal to friendship here draws on certain strands of the feminist 'ethic of care' which holds that we should begin from a vision of the public as antecedently relational. Thus:

> A society that took caring seriously would engage in a discussion of the issues of public life from a vision not of autonomous, equal, rational actors each pursuing separate ends, but from a vision of interdependent actors, each of whom needs and provides care in a variety of ways and each of whom has other interests and pursuits that exist outside of the realm of care. (Tronto, 1993, 168)

The idea is that it may be a mistake to think of community as a coming together of individuals who would have remained separate were it not for the fact that they had struck upon, or been given, some deep moral reason for associating together. On the contrary, it might make more sense for us to think of liberal political community as one particular configuration of a group of people who are already, and basically, related as friends.

In this way, the friendship paradigm puts Kukathas's contention that community is conditional on agreement to the question. If friendship is basic, then it does not presuppose agreement and is not necessarily defeated by the absence of agreement. Consequently, the friendship paradigm seems to suggest an account of social unity capable of surviving in conditions of moral conflict, which, as I suggested at the outset, is precisely what the liberal advocate of political community needs. It is my belief that friendship provides the answer we are looking for, but clearly the claim stands in need of further articulation and defence. I shall devote the rest of this chapter to the clarification of my appeal to friendship and then, in the final chapter, I shall seek to defend the claim from a number of rather serious objections.

Friendship and properties

Friendship seems to provide a response to the problem of liberal community because it suggests a form of companionship that is *basic*.[2]

The suggestion is that our friends are people we just do care about – it is inappropriate to suppose that friendship can be explained in terms of something else. This understanding of friendship brings it within the domain of love as Harry Frankfurt characterizes it when writing of the love of parents for their children:

> I can declare with unequivocal confidence that I do not love my children because I am aware of some value that inheres in them independent of my love for them. The fact is that I loved them even before they were born – before I had any especially relevant information about their personal characteristics or their particular merits and virtues. (Frankfurt, 2004, 39)

Frankfurt's assertion is that we do not love things because we antecedently deem them to be valuable; the relationship runs in the opposite direction: 'what we love necessarily acquires value for us because we love it' (Frankfurt, 2004, 39). Love is, in this sense, basic. Now it is true that Frankfurt appeals here to a very intimate relation of love – the love of parents for their children – but he is clear that the range of objects of this sort of basic love is actually very broad including persons, countries, traditions, social justice, scientific truth and so on (Frankfurt, 2004, 41). The kind of friendship I have in mind will fall within this range, and thus we may properly speak of one's love for one's friends. And, if one's love for one's friends is basic in this sense, there is reason, on the face of it, to think that friendship, unlike citizenship as I have characterized it, could survive in conditions of conflict.

However, one might question the claim that friendship is basic. One might argue that friendship is appropriately conceived as an 'object-centred' relationship (Kahane, 1999, 269–73). This view of friendship holds that we are attracted to our friends because (and only because) they possess some property that we value: I care about you *because* you make me laugh; or *because* you are very confident; or *because* you are an honest and generous person. Moreover, should you cease to display these friendship-inducing properties, I shall cease to care about you. Clearly it is important for my argument that friendship is not, or at least need not be, like this; if friendship is always explicable by reference to the properties of the friend, then it is not basic in the required sense and the friendship paradigm seems liable to collapse into the citizenship paradigm. The critic might object that we are only friends with people with whom we share a substantial scheme of values or a conception of the good life. In other words, in order to be friends, we must first conceive of ourselves as sharing in a pilgrimage, an escape or a quest. Kahane attributes this view to Aristotle for whom he suggests that 'it is common features of character that draw us together' as friends (Kahane, 1999, 271). And, indeed, there are a number of theorists who have argued that loving attachments are entirely explicable in terms of the properties of the beloved (Delaney, 1996; Levine, 1999; Keller 2000).

But I do not think it must be this way. There is in my view a very significant difference between the friendship and citizenship paradigms and it turns on the idea that friendship, unlike citizenship, can be an attachment that is basic and that is not explicable (certainly not fully explicable) by appeal to the properties of the friend. Certainly it seems that any extreme interpretation of the properties-based view of friendship is going to be untenable. At the level of personal friendship, at least, it is just implausible to claim that I care about my friend only because he displays certain properties: he is clever, he makes me laugh, he is a congenial companion. For what if he stopped displaying those properties? Am I to suppose that I should stop caring for him at that point? Perhaps I would, but supposing that I did not, I do not think it plausible to suggest that I had made any sort of mistake. The bond of friendship is surely stronger, more forgiving and less rigid than this rather crude version of the properties account would imply.

But the properties-theorist might very well insist that I have misrepresented her claim. The idea is not that I care for my friends on the basis of a 'shopping list' of qualities; the idea is simply that friendship is *in principle* explicable by appeal to the properties of the friends. For example, then, whether I recognize it or not – and perhaps I do not – I care about Eduardo because (and ultimately only because) we share certain understandings about the good life. Were either of us to undergo a transformation of our view of the good life, the friendship would necessarily come to an end. There is no requirement here that this be a conscious process. I do not have to be constantly testing my friendships against a checklist of criteria for the properties account of friendship to be true. As I have elsewhere suggested, very often 'we have no idea why we feel as we do; very often we claim to love the beloved for properties he or she does not in fact possess. None of this means that love is not based upon properties; all it means is that love is mysterious' (Edyvane, 2003, 63).

Nevertheless, I think there are other reasons to doubt that the properties account is true in all cases. A further difficulty is suggested by Susan Mendus:

> If I now claim to be committed to my husband I precisely cannot give an exhaustive account of the characteristics he possesses in virtue of which I have that commitment to him: if I could do so, there would be a real question as to why I am not prepared to show the same commitment to another person who shares those characteristics (his twin brother, for example). (Mendus, 2001, 75)

If my friendship for Eduardo is entirely explicable in terms of our shared conception of the good life, why is it that I do not feel for everybody else who shares my conception of the good life the same as I feel for Eduardo? Perhaps we might say that I care more for Eduardo than for others because, in addition to his views about the good life, I value a number of his other properties that distinguish him from all the other people who share only my views about the good life. I shall never meet somebody who possesses exactly the same qualities as Eduardo and that is why I care more about him than anybody else. But I do not think that this response will suffice, for it cannot explain why I would not be prepared to care in the same way for an exactly identical other *should one come along.* Even though we will never be confronted with the choice, it remains important to us to believe that we would not be so prepared (Edyvane, 2003, 63).

The implication is that some loves, and I think some friendships too, are basic in the sense that it would be implausible to try to explain them in terms of something 'deeper' than the relationship itself. Montaigne appeals to the quality I have in mind when he writes of his friendship with Etienne de La Boetie that if 'you press me to tell why I loved him, I feel that this cannot be expressed, except by answering: Because it was he, because it was I'

(Montaigne, 1991, 192). It is relationships like these that I mean to designate with the term 'friendship', and it is relationships like these that I believe hold the key to a liberal political community. For a relationship that is basic in this way, which does not depend upon the existence of some antecedent agreement with respect to the good, is a relationship that need not be undermined by the conflicts which characterize liberal democratic societies. *Pace* Kukathas, it is not the understandings they share that make a community of friends.

Friendship and journeys

The move to the friendship paradigm has quite a profound affect on the way in which we understand the journey narratives I have examined in this study. The friendship paradigm essentially *inverts* the citizenship paradigm. On the latter, we are companions because we share a life as pilgrims, as escapees or as questers. We think of ourselves as sharing a life in community because we share an understanding of the shape that the enterprise ought to take. On the former, by contrast, we share a life as pilgrims, escapees or questers because we antecedently view ourselves as companions. Shared interests and values are not a presupposition of friendship, but a consequence of it. And this seems a natural way of thinking about friendship and the kind of love it involves.

This possibility is well illustrated in John Steinbeck's novel, *Of Mice and Men*. The novel tells the tale of George and Lennie who 'travel together' in search of work (Steinbeck, 1995, 27). It is clear, however, that they do not travel together because they antecedently share an interest. George plainly states that his interests as an individual are not consonant with the journey he shares with Lennie:

> God a'mighty, if I was alone I could live so easy. I could go get a job an' work, an' no trouble. No mess at all, and when the end of the month come I could take my fifty bucks and go into town and get whatever I want. Why, I could stay in a cat-house all night. I could eat any place I want, hotel or any place, and order any damn thing I could think of. An' I could do all that every damn month. Get a gallon of whisky, or set in a pool room and

play cards or shoot pool. ... An' whatta I got? ... I got you! You can't keep a job and you lose me ever' job I get. Ju's keep me shovin' all over the country all the time. (Steinbeck, 1995, 12)

Evidently, George and Lennie do not travel together for the sake of their mutual advantage or because of some antecedent agreement with respect to the good life. They travel together simply because they are friends. But, in and through their friendship, they form a distinct set of shared interests and a shared goal which involves the abandonment of George's individual interest. We can see this as George repeats to Lennie the best-laid plan they have come to share which he has articulated 'many times before' (Steinbeck, 1995, 14):

'OK. Some day – we're gonna get the jack together and we're gonna have a little house and a couple of acres an' a cow and some pigs and ...'

'*An' live off the fatta the lan'*,' Lennie shouted. 'An' have *rabbits*. Go on George! Tell about what we're gonna have in the garden and about the rabbits in the cages and about the rain in the winter and the stove, and how thick the cream is on the milk like you can hardly cut it. Tell about that, George.' (Steinbeck, 1995, 15)

Because the shape of George and Lennie's journey is a consequence of the fact that they travel together and not a presupposition of it, their companionship is not conditional on the reality of the shared dream that structures their association. In other words, while the shape of their companionship would certainly change, it would not necessarily be negated by the realization that they never really would have a little house and 'live off the fatta the lan'. It is their basic friendship and not their shared dream that holds them together.

We can now see that the friendship paradigm gestures towards a very different way of thinking about the quest narrative I discussed in the previous chapter. The case for the quest model rather fell apart when it became apparent that the Holy Grail was not really a plausible object upon which to pin our collective hopes. I suggested that in the conditions of a modern society, it is very hard to develop and sustain a faith that the Grail of a common good is really out there somewhere for us to discover. The worry was that by conceiving of ourselves as sharing with our fellow citizens in a quest for the Grail, we revealed ourselves to be as crazy as Don Quixote. But perhaps we might now retrace our steps. The procedural community looked like an accurate representation of the kinds of communities we know in modern life and seemed to provide a picture of political community congenial to liberalism. The trouble began with the communitarian objection, voiced by Miller, that a shared life structured by nothing but devotion to procedures would be meaningless. As a response to this charge, I invoked the device of the Grail as a relatively non-comprehensive way of investing the shared life of a procedural community with meaning. But perhaps at this point we would have done well to heed the advice of David Wiggins when he suggests that we go wrong in the very question, 'What is *the* meaning of life?' Or, indeed, 'What is *the* meaning of a shared life?':

> We bewitch ourselves to think we are looking for some one thing like the Garden of the Hesperides, the Holy Grail... Then finding nothing like that in the world ... we console ourselves by looking inwards, but again for some one substitute thing, one thing in us now instead of the world. ... [But,] it would be better to go back to the 'the' in the original question; and to interest ourselves afresh in what everybody knows about – the set of concerns he actually has (Wiggins, 1987, 136).

The meaningfulness of a shared life need not be pinned to some abstract Holy Grail somewhere just beyond the horizon, but to the journey itself the meaningfulness of which, 'so far from having nowhere to go but round and round in circles, fans out into a whole arborescence of concerns' (Wiggins, 1987, 101).

This remark calls to mind Walt Whitman's 'Song of the Open Road'. The road is open and the journey has no particular goal, but it would be a mistake to infer from this that the journey is meaningless. Whitman rejoices in the journey itself, a life-long voyage which ends only in death:

> Afoot and light-hearted, I take to the open road,
> Healthy, free, the world before me,
> The long brown path before me, leading wherever I choose.
> (Whitman, 1990, 120)

For Whitman, the journey has a great deal to recommend it. He writes of freedom ('I ordain myself loos'd of limits and imaginary lines'), heroism and creativity ('I think heroic deeds were all conceiv'd in the open air, and all great poems also'), self-discovery ('I am larger, better than I thought'), self-realization ('here is a man tallied – he realizes here what he has in him'), companionship ('Allons! Whoever you are, come travel with me!), and of other divine things 'well envelop'd' and 'more beautiful than words can tell' (Whitman, 1990, 122–5). In other words, the journey reveals a whole 'arborescence' of concerns. And, of course, this is the moral of so many quest stories. This is the central ambiguity I mentioned in the previous chapter: 'the quester pursues a goal with compulsive devotion, but the very act of pursuing it becomes his primary value' (Stout, 1983, 91). Ultimately, on this interpretation of the quest, it is not the journey's end that matters; if you were expecting to find a pot of gold (or some such) at the end of the rainbow, then nothing awaits you but disappointment. Unlike consumers and citizens, who do pin their hopes on the pot of gold, friends are able to say that it was the shared journey that really mattered and not the destination. Only friends are able to say of their shared life that it was better to travel than to arrive. As C.P. Cavafy has it in his poem 'Ithaca':

And if you find her poor, Ithaca has not defrauded you.
With the great wisdom you have gained, with so much experience,
you must surely have understood by then what Ithacas mean.
(Cavafy, 1976, 61)

Thus, there need be nothing crazy about Don Quixote's quest if we read it as a story of his friendship with Sancho Panza.[3]

In other words, then, my suggestion is that the appropriate response to the communitarian objection we encountered in the previous chapter is not to suggest that a shared commitment to liberal procedures is a meaningful focus for community because those procedures are instrumental to the realization of some common good, whether it be known, unknown, positive or negative. Rather, the procedural community is meaningful because the liberal procedures that provide its focus are regarded as the *expression* of an antecedent and basic bond and concern between the members of the association. In this way, it is possible for the procedural community to be a meaningful community even though it may not serve to realize any common good at all. This is why the journey of Monsignor Quixote and Sancho is meaningful in spite of their recognition that their enterprise lacks any significant purpose.

Now all of this might prompt the feeling that, on the friendship paradigm, the question of the journey's shape, which has occupied so much of our attention to this point, is reduced to an after-thought. If companionship is not conditional on the particular kind of journey we conceive ourselves as taking, then it may seem not to matter what shape our shared life happens to possess. But I do not think that that is quite right. In fact, there are several very impor-tant interrelationships to be noted between the shape of one's journey and the character of the companionship it involves. Certainly, my claim is that the shared life is to be regarded as prior to the shape it possesses, but that does not entail that the shape is unimportant. I think this for two reasons. First, we should not forget that we are still concerned to provide an account of a *liberal* community. Communities of friends need not, I think, possess a liberal shape. For example, a community of friends could plausibly take on the shape of an escape; and, as we have seen, escape shaped communities are not distinctively liberal. Consequently, my argu-ment to this point still applies. It seems to me that a plausibly liberal community of friends would have to possess the shape of an escape that merges into quest, a quest incorporating the refinements I have suggested in this section. The appropriate shape, in other words, is not so much that of the medieval Grail-quest, but rather that of the modern road-trip: a quest without the promise, or even the likelihood, of a Grail.

I also think that the journey's shape matters to the character of the companionship it displays notwithstanding the primacy of friendship. Just because we are friends and companions before we are escapees, for instance, it does not mean that coming to conceive of ourselves as sharing in an escape will not have some significant impact on the character of our relationships with one another. Clearly Hazel and Fiver in *Watership Down* were friends before they embarked on their escape, but it would be absurd to suggest that the escape they shared had no impact on the character of their relation-ship. It is a commonplace in both literature and life that friendships are at their most intense when times are hard, and conversely it is perhaps harder to sustain friendships when our shared lives lack any particular direction. Shapes can help to structure, consolidate and extend the shared lives they outline. They might be secondary to the shared life itself, but they are nevertheless still critical to our understanding of liberal community.

But the interrelation here also runs in the opposite direction: the nature of the companionship of fellow travellers seems liable to affect, to at least some extent, the shape of the journey they conceive of themselves as undertaking. Where companionship has or assumes the form of friendship, the journey, whatever its shape may be, seems likely to become more like a quest in the sense in which I have described it in this section. That is to say, if I am or come to be friends with my fellow pilgrims, then it will begin to matter less to me whether we reach the shrine we were pursuing. Indeed, I may even begin to fear the journey's end; I may yearn for it to persist for as long as possible. Similarly, if I am or come to be friends with my fellow escapees, then the evils we resist seem likely to lose some of their centrality as we begin to realize other values – the values of friendship – in the journey itself. The general point I am trying to emphasize here is that a complete picture of political community seems to require an appreciation of three key elements: the shape of the shared life, the character of the companionship between those who share the life, and an understanding of the interplay of shape and companionship in this context.

Friendship and community

The move to the friendship paradigm transforms not only the way in which we think about the journey narratives that I have discussed in this book, but also the way in which we approach the question of community in contemporary political philosophy. As I suggested in Chapter 1, most accounts of community in the literature operate on the belief that we must locate sources of commonality in the political society in order to ground and explain social unity. Liberals who worry about coercion seek to *discover* the understandings we share: Mason suggests that we might share an understanding of the value of the polity; Stout argues that we might converge on a provisional conception of the good; Stephen Macedo thinks that most of us might even agree on certain comprehensive liberal values, like autonomy. Nationalists and some comprehensive liberals like Galston take a different approach. These theorists are more willing to *invent* commonality through the various processes of moral education. Kukathas, by contrast again, simply supposes that there is no significant commonality to be discovered or invented by acceptable means, and so regards any 'deep' form of community as unattainable. In his view, political community 'will have to be regarded, ethically speaking, as a far less significant construct than many have suggested' (Kukathas, 2003, 181).

There is clearly a great deal of disagreement between these authors, but it is notable that, beneath their differences, there is one fundamental issue upon which they do all seem to concur. They all agree that community is ultimately grounded in commonality and shared understanding: 'the greater the diversity of cultural groups with independent moral traditions within a polity, the less the extent of social unity within that political society' (Kukathas, 2003, 166). Kukathas presents this as a strict and self-evident logical relationship, and certainly it seems to be a guiding conviction of those theorists who seek to provide an account of liberal political community.

The move to the friendship paradigm is dramatic in this intellectual context, then, because it casts the whole approach and basic assumptions of these theorists into doubt. It raises the unsettling possibility that we have been going about the problem of community in entirely the wrong way. From the perspective of the friendship paradigm, the standard approach seems back-to-front. On the friendship view, it is just not clear that there is much to be gained by inquiring into the possible bases of agreement in a modern democratic society. On the friendship view, commonality and shared purposes are a consequence of community and not a presupposition. It may thus be a mistake to suppose that we can plausibly explain communal warmth and solidarity between citizens by appeal to the understandings they share. The philosophical task on the friendship paradigm is to articulate and defend the concept of friendship, to show that it provides a plausible interpretation of the solidarity found in a liberal polity. The political task is to foster and promote among citizens the capacity and disposition to care for each other. It is far from clear that the articulation of shared understandings is going to be of any assistance in either of these tasks.

There is a positive side to this, however. The friendship paradigm suggests that we should not be disheartened by the failure to locate any significant sources of commonality in the modern democratic society, because there is no reason to suppose that such commonality is necessary for community. If we are friends, then the fact that we disagree sharply about the good life, about religion, about nationality need not matter. We care about each other, and so we stick together.

Now, I have suggested that the friendship paradigm cuts against the approach of most contemporary liberal political philosophy, but I want to finish this chapter by identifying one very striking and quite remarkable exception to this: John Rawls. Rawls's account, in *A Theory of Justice*, of the social union of a well-ordered liberal society certainly regards community as being expressed in a shared commitment to the principles of justice, but it is less clear that he regards the community as being *explained* by that shared commitment, much less by a shared understanding with respect to the common good. The shared commitment to the principles of justice comes about as the culmination of a motivational story of moral development central to which are bonds of care and friendship. As Rawls explains, his account of the development of morality 'supposes that affection for particular people plays an essential part in the acquisition of morality' (Rawls, 1999, 426). The commitment to principles of justice for their own sake, which Rawls calls the 'morality of principles', is presented as a natural extension of our basic concern for those with whom we associate:

We may suppose that there is a morality of association in which the members of society view one another as equals, as friends and associates, joined together in a system of cooperation known to be for the advantage of all and governed by a common conception of justice. The content of this morality is characterized by the cooperative virtues: those of justice and fairness, fidelity and trust, integrity and impartiality. The typical vices are graspingness and unfairness, dishonesty and deceit, prejudice and bias. ... These moral attitudes are bound to exist once we become attached to those cooperating with us in a just (or fair) scheme. (Rawls, 1999, 413)

While Rawls is clear that this 'morality of association' is, in some sense, transcended as the final stage of moral development, the morality of principles, is reached, he is also clear that the attitudes of care and concern which constitute the earlier stage are likely to be 'to some degree necessary' for later moral motivation (Rawls, 1999, 426). Now, it is not altogether clear precisely how he thinks these attitudes might be necessary, but what I really mean to emphasize here is the order of explanation. Shared commitment to the principles of justice is not portrayed here as the *source* of social unity as theorists have often suggested (Miller, 1989, 60; Kymlicka, 1996, 187), but as the *consequence* of prior association. The emphasis of Rawls's motivational account, and of his story of moral development in particular, is of the way in which our commitment to the principles of justice can be seen to emerge from, and to be enriched by, an antecedent, and basic, concern we have for those with whom we associate.

This is a point that has been emphasized by Susan Mendus, who finds in Rawls's motivational account a source of support for her contention that 'our partial concerns provide impartial morality with its motivational foundation' (Mendus, 2002, 157). To be sure, this is not the standard reading of Rawls, but it is a reading rather well supported by the text – we would have to ignore the vast majority of Part III of *A Theory of Justice* if we were to suggest in any seriousness that partial concerns, and, specifically, basic partial concern for one's fellow citizens, had no significant role to play in Rawls's ideal of the well-ordered society. For the time being I mean only to flag this apparent exception to the general view of community in the theoretical literature, but I shall return to the case of Rawls in the next chapter and provide some further discussion of his view and of the way in which it appears to appeal to something like the idea of friendship.

My concern in this section has been to consider what impact the move to the friendship paradigm has upon the way in which contemporary political philosophy approaches the question of community. In this connection, I have made two claims. First, I have suggested that the move to the friendship paradigm indicates that the preoccupation of liberal theorists with the relation between community and conflict, and particularly the notion that the two stand in an inverse relation (the greater the conflict, the more attenuated the community), could be misguided. The friendship paradigm suggests that conflict is not necessarily a barrier to community. Where the bond of community is understood as a form of friendship, community is not conditional on consensus. For this reason, the search for shared understandings might be needless. Secondly, I have tried to show that the importance I am attaching to friendship as a political concept is not altogether unprecedented and can be seen to have a more established place in liberal political philosophy. In particular, I have noted the manner in which John Rawls's account of the well-ordered society seems to acknowledge an important role for attachments of basic care and concern among citizens.

Summary

In this chapter, I have tried to articulate a way of thinking about the nature of attachment, or companionship, in the shared life of a political community that diverges quite fundamentally from the conventional view to be found in the literature. The conventional view holds that we share a life in political community as fellow citizens because we antecedently regard ourselves as sharing a conception of the good or the bad or the process which will shape our collective undertaking. By presenting the order of explanation in this way, with solidarity as a consequence of agreement, the conventional approach is rendered inhospitable to pluralism. We have reason to exhibit solidarity only in so far as we agree with our fellow citizens about the purposes of the polity. The approach that I have articulated seeks to reverse this order of explanation. On the friendship paradigm, any agreement about processes or purposes is conceived as a consequence of prior solidarity or friendship. Friendship here is conceived as a basic attachment, which means that it cannot be explained in terms of something 'deeper' like the properties of the friend. For this reason, the bond of friendship suggests the possibility that a distinctively liberal form of political community might yet be capable of surviving in conditions of pronounced moral conflict.

But, of course, there is considerable uneasiness here, which I have so far quite deliberately set aside. Perhaps there is a very good reason for the neglect of an argument that suggests that the members of modern democratic societies should all just be friends with one another. Certainly, there are many reasons to doubt the plausibility of friendship as the source of liberal solidarity. As I observed earlier, Monsignor Quixote's response to Sancho – 'I suppose – friendship?' – is deeply tentative, as is the rest of their conversation:

'Is that enough?'
'We will find out in time.' (Greene, 2000, 44)

In the next, and final, chapter I shall consider and answer what I take to be the three most fundamental objections to the idea of friendship as a political relationship.

7
Political Friendship

I have argued that the bond of friendship provides the most promising source of the solidarity of a liberal political community in conditions of pronounced moral conflict. We share the 'open road' of a political life with our fellow citizens because we care about them at a basic level. In some sense, we regard them as our friends. But as I noted at the end of the last chapter, that seems a very strong claim indeed. On the face of it, the bond of friendship does not seem a particularly plausible candidate for the bond of a vast modern society whose members do not know each other, do not like each other and do not agree with each other about the substantive direction they would like their shared life to take. In this chapter, I will defend my appeal to friendship and argue that it can plausibly constitute the bond of a society with the characteristics I have mentioned. Indeed, I hope to show that friendship might in fact provide a *more* plausible interpretation of liberal solidarity than does the prevailing 'citizenship' approach, which conceives of community as grounded in commonality.

In order to vindicate the appeal to friendship, I shall respond to what I take to be the three most fundamental challenges to the coherence of my thesis. The chapter is therefore divided into three sections. The first section is devoted to what I shall term the problem of *projection*.[1] The charge here is that the idea of friendship projected onto the modern state is simply unintelligible. Friendship is a fundamentally personal relationship and is entirely meaningless at the level of a modern society. The second section is devoted to what I shall term the problem of *subversion*. The charge here is that friendship cannot serve as the bond of a liberal political community because it is inherently subversive of liberal values. Friendship is far too capricious and partial a relationship to provide a stable basis for a liberal society. The third section is devoted to what I regard as the most serious objection, which I shall term the problem of *motivation*. The charge here is that there is something corrupt about the idea that we could be friends with our moral and political adversaries. Caring about such people appears to constitute an offence against our own moral and political beliefs and so some account is required to explain why we should see such people as friends.

Projection

My discussion of friendship in the previous chapter appealed to examples of personal friendship, romantic love and the love of parents for their children. I suggested that in such cases, it made sense to think of the concern involved as basic. Such relationships, I argued, are not usually conditional on the properties of the parties involved and it is thus inappropriate to suppose that the bond might be explained in terms of something else, such as agreement with respect to the good. Our friends are people we just do care about. And this feature of friendship, I suggested, should be very appealing to the political theorist of community, for it suggests the possibility of a community of friends, a community capable of flourishing even where the parties involved disagree about the good life and substantial moral matters. But of course all of this is vulnerable to one rather straightforward and apparently fatal objection: attachments which are basic in this way are invariably very intimate attachments. It is only our concern for our very closest friends and family which displays this kind of unconditionality, and there is no way of projecting the idea onto the modern state.

Sandra Marshall voices this objection when she writes that one 'of the important claims of justice and rights is that they apply to everyone; is it *really* possible for me to be a friend to everyone? Such an idea may seem to make no sense' (Marshall, 1998, 216). The last sentence here is important; the charge is not that this sort of projection of friendship is impractical, but that it is (or may be) *unintelligible*. 'Friendship, however circumscribed by context, is still a *personal* relationship, and as such it just cannot fit into many of the transactions and dealings which we have with others' (Marshall, 1998, 216; see also Kahane, 1999, 276). Modern societies are vast and complex (indeed, they are vastly complex). We have no contact with the overwhelming majority of our 'fellow' citizens; it would be absurd to regard these people as our friends. And it is worth adding here that the problem of projection is nothing new; it is as old as Aristotle. Aristotle was deeply pessimistic about the possibility, suggested by Plato in the *Republic*, of projecting any intimate model of friendship onto the larger society. He felt that the projection would inevitably involve a dilution of the attachment to the extent that the attachment would cease to obtain. He likened this process to the way in which 'a little sweet wine mingled with a great deal of water is imperceptible in the mixture' (Aristotle, 1984, 1262b15–25). If the idea of personal friendship on a political scale was hard to comprehend in the context of the ancient Athenian city-state, then in the context of modernity it is liable to be found altogether meaningless.

Of course, any response to the problem of projection would have to concede that the bond of political friendship is going to be quite different from the bond of personal friendship. Our personal friends are people we know very well and they are people we like very much. It would be entirely implausible to defend a view of political community whose members were attached in such an intimate way. But it is not clear that we have to think of friendship in quite such a sentimental manner. While Aristotle was sceptical about the projection of very intimate, familial relations onto the larger society, he nevertheless held that the political community was a community of friends of a sort. Alasdair MacIntyre suggests that part of the problem for us is that the modern understanding of friendship has become extremely etiolated. As he explains, in 'a modern perspective, affection is often the central issue; our friends are said to be those whom we *like*, perhaps whom we like very much. "Friendship" has become for the most part the name of a type of emotional state' (MacIntyre, 1985, 156). For the ancient Greeks, by contrast, 'friendship' (*philia*) was a far richer notion which encompassed a broader range of attachments; it was the name not of an emotional state, but of 'a type of social and political relationship' (MacIntyre, 1985, 156). While the kind of political friendship I have in mind is not readily captured by any of the species delineated by Aristotle, I do wish to emphasize the more general point that there might be more to friendship than the sentimental intimacy we moderns tend to associate with the term.[2]

But, then, we might reasonably inquire as to just what is meant here by political friendship. I want to suggest that political friendship is a form of political relationship characterized by a basic (non-property-based) concern for the other. Is it plausible to suggest that we could be concerned for all of our fellow citizens? It seems to me that it is. Certainly it is possible to be concerned for a person one does not like: I am concerned for the students I teach, I want them to succeed in their studies, achieve good degrees and live happy lives, and I am willing to make certain personal sacrifices in order to promote their flourishing. I do not necessarily (or indeed, often) *like* them or feel *affectionate* towards them. In fact, my being concerned for them is entirely compatible with my positively *disliking* them. There is no straightforward correspondence between care and concern on the one hand, and affection on the other. Nor, I think, is there any requirement that I must personally know those for whom I am concerned. I might be concerned for the fate of a group of people involved in a train crash even though I have not the faintest idea of their identities. Surely one can 'imagine' political friendship in much the same way as one can imagine community. The idea is essentially that I *presume* political friendship with my fellow citizens.

And this is surely not an unfamiliar notion. According to Aristotle, one can see 'in one's travels how near and dear a thing every man is to every other' (Aristotle, 1976, 1155a21). Of course, the concern involved here will not be as intense, intimate or sentimental as that we might expect between personal friends, but many of the same values could plausibly be thought to structure the relationship. We might say that our default disposition towards strangers is one of 'friendliness'. For example, I may not feel any personal affection for the stranger I pass in the street, yet I might very well not wish to profit at her expense by pocketing the purse she had unwittingly dropped (as I would not wish to profit at the expense of my personal friends); I might very well not wish to see her in any distress and would seek to help her if she fell (as I would for my friends). And, importantly, I might well regard my pocketing the purse or my failure to help as a form of *betrayal*. Perhaps we might think that 'betrayal' is too strong a term in this context, but surely the idea of 'letting down' is not. In the same way as I would feel that I had let my friend down if I failed to go to his aid when he needed it, I might well feel that I had let the stranger down by neglecting to help her. It is not absurd to suppose that this feeling, the feeling of having let the stranger down, could be prompted by the sense that one had failed to live up to the standards of political friendship. There is nothing unintelligible about the suggestion that I could be concerned for the 'weal and woe' of those around me, even where I neither know them nor like them (Marshall, 1998, 217). Indeed, it is a common phenomenon.

However, the critic might persist that the problem of projection does not turn crucially on the possibility of one's being concerned for one's fellow citizens. Far more troubling is the other part of my formulation, the suggestion that relations of political friendship should be *basic*: the idea that one might be *non-conditionally* concerned for one's fellow citizens is extremely difficult to comprehend. It seems to be one thing to suggest that I might be concerned for my fellow citizens in so far as I believe that we share an ethically substantive national identity or conception of the good life, quite another to suggest that these could be people who, like my closest personal friends, I just *do* care about. But that is precisely what I want to claim. In fact, I want to suggest that it is actually more plausible to suppose that our commitment to our fellow citizens is basic than it is to suppose that it is conditional on some sort of commonality. The support for this claim comes from the evidence of our experience, which I discussed at some length in the Introduction.

It seems to me that basic, non-conditional concern for others is far more widespread than we are often inclined to think. When I give up my seat on a train for another person in need, I do not think that my so doing is conditional on our sharing fundamental values or a common national identity; I do it *just because* I am concerned for this person's weal and woe. When I place my trust in strangers and when I reward the trust they place in me, I have no further reason for trusting or being trustworthy beyond the fact that I am concerned for them. Perhaps the clearest example once again is given by the case of blood donation. Because it is voluntary, anonymous and freely given, it is implausible to claim that such behaviour expresses anything other than basic, non-conditional concern for those around oneself. Liberal nationalists sometimes argue that in order plausibly to explain commitment to the political institutions of a welfare state, it must be the case that citizens subject to those institutions share a national identity (Miller, 1989, 60; Tamir, 1993, 117–21). But why could it not be the case that we endorse significant redistribution simply because we are basically concerned for others? Why must we appeal to commonality at all?

It may come as a surprise, but it seems that many of us are basically concerned for the weal and woe of those around us, our political friends. Far from being unintelligible, political friendship seems to provide the most plausible interpretation of the reality of our lives. Of course projection involves a degree of dilution: political friendship is not the same as personal friendship, and a good thing too. But the two nevertheless share certain fundamental characteristics; both forms of relationship can involve basic, non-conditional concern for the other.

Subversion

Political friendship may be an intelligible concept, but that does not mean that it necessarily constitutes the most appropriate social bond of a liberal community. The strong charge here, which I mean to designate with the idea of 'subversion', is that friendship is an *intrinsically illiberal* attachment and that, consequently, it is necessarily subverting of the liberal political order. Why should we think that? Well, in the modern discourse, the association of politics and friendship often has a rather negative sense. We can be very suspicious of the suggestion that friendship should play a significant role in politics, and for two main reasons. The first is that concern for one's friends is a form of partiality, and yet it is typically felt that the appropriate bond of a liberal society should be one characterized by impartiality. The appeal to friendship in politics is liable to be associated with the dangers of nepotism, corruption and bias. Liberalism is a politics of impartiality, whereas friendship necessarily seems to generate a politics of partiality. Consequently, it is thought that friendship is necessarily subverting of the liberal impartial order. The second major concern about friendship in politics is that it is simply not a very sturdy relationship. Friendships come and go; they are (or can be) fragile relations easily defeated, and, as such, do not seem to provide a particularly stable or predictable basis for any political order, let alone a liberal order in which conflict is rife.

In this section, I shall offer a response to both of these worries. But my strategy will not be to show that political friendship will not subvert the liberal political order. It seems to me that it might. I think it would be implausible to suggest that friendship cannot become subversive. Rather, I shall aim to deny the strong claim that political friendship is *intrinsically* subversive. My strategy will be to show that friendship need not undermine the liberal political order.

So, the first concern is that political friendship is a partial attachment and must therefore undermine the impartiality of a liberal political order. The worry here is that if we are all friends, then I might favour my closer political friends at the expense of my more distant political friends. From a liberal point of view this is troubling, but from the point of view of the (partial) morality of friendship it is entirely legitimate and, in fact, to be encouraged. Martin Hollis writes that 'it would be hard to find a neater definition of corruption in public life. Good citizenship is precisely not using one's offices for the benefit of one's friends' (Hollis, 1996a, 165). But note that the worry here rests upon a very stark distinction between the morality of friendship and the morality of impartiality. It is not necessarily, or not always, true that from the perspective of friendship it is entirely legitimate to favour one's closer friends ahead of one's more distant friends. In the previous chapter, I noted Rawls's suggestion that our attachments of care and concern might even serve to lead us into a commitment to impartial morality.

It is easier to see this if we start at the other end. That is to say, would it really be absurd for a person to claim that she was committed to the liberal polity and the (impartial) morality it embodies *out of* her basic concern for others? It seems to me that it would not. Jason Scorza observes that friends often disagree with one another, but notes that in contrast to 'unfriendly' disagreements,

> friends try to govern their disagreements in such a way as to preserve and develop, rather than terminate the bond between them. They do not excessively stifle or suppress disagreements, creating deadly silences that could cause the bonds of friendship to gradually erode. Nor do they engage in unrestrained free-for-alls, risking the eruption of violence that could cause the

bonds of friendship to suddenly snap. ... One might say that friends try to disagree today in a manner that will allow them to disagree again tomorrow. (Scorza, 2004, 90)

Scorza implies, not implausibly, that built into the value of friendship is a concern to perpetuate the relationship, to find some way of getting along without altogether silencing the disagreements that could potentially tear the relationship apart. The suggestion is that it is a central requirement and concern of friendship that we find some way of living together today that will allow us to continue living together tomorrow. And if this is true of personal friendships, then it will certainly be true of political friendships within which we might sensibly expect disagreement to be all the more pronounced. I emphasize this feature of friendship because it seems reasonable to regard the liberal polity and the liberal morality as answering to that concern. Surely one of the central inspirations of political liberalism is its concern to articulate a way in which a group of people who disagree with one another can continue living together in relative peace and unity without altogether silencing the disagreement between them. Thus, a person might reasonably say that she was committed to the liberal polity and its impartial morality out of her concern to perpetuate her relationship with her political friends. Far from undermining the bonds of political friendship, it seems that, by providing a framework for social unity in conditions of conflict, impartial political morality might actually support them.

More substantially, Rawls makes the striking suggestion that we could plausibly regard the requirements of a specifically *egalitarian* liberal political morality as the expression of antecedent political friendship. In the previous chapter, I noted the manner in which Rawls's motivational account of the sense of justice regarded friendship – the morality of association – as constituting a stage on the road to a complete sense of justice. An implication of this, as Mendus observes, is the supposition on Rawls's part that 'the positive value we find in associating with others ... need not be undermined by commitment to impartial morality' (Mendus, 2002, 78). In Part I of *A Theory of Justice*, Rawls makes the even stronger claim that commitment to his 'difference principle', which states that social and economic inequalities are to be arranged so that they are to the greatest benefit of the least advantaged (Rawls, 1999, 266), can plausibly be thought to express a sense of 'fraternity' among citizens. He writes:

> Members of a family commonly do not wish to gain unless they can do so in ways that further the interests of the rest. Now wanting to act on the difference principle has precisely this consequence. Those better circumstanced are willing to have their greater advantages only under a scheme in which this works out for the benefit of the less fortunate. (Rawls, 1999, 90)

This remark seems to confirm the claim I made in the previous chapter that Rawls does not seek to explain social unity by reference to the shared commitment to principles of justice. On the contrary, the passage just quoted suggests that the principles of justice are to be regarded as the expression of an antecedent, and quite deep, mutuality. Rawls characterizes this mutuality as 'fraternity', but it seems to me that 'friendship' might in fact be more fitting. Fraternity implies an involuntary form of association that is rather at odds with the general liberal tenor of Rawls's account, which holds that in 'justice as fairness men *agree* to share one another's fate' (Rawls, 1971, 102, my emphasis). Brothers, we might think, share each other's fate whether they like it or not. In any case, the general idea I mean to emphasize here is that a measure of basic concern for one's fellow citizens, far from subverting the political order, might in some cases promote the endorsement of liberal egalitarian redistributive principles.

So, my claim is that political friendship is not intrinsically undermining of the liberal political order. I have defended this claim by arguing that it would not be implausible for a person to say that she was committed to the liberal political morality *out of* concern for her political friends. It would not be implausible for her to make this suggestion because it seems a reasonable view of friendship to suppose that it involves, minimally, the concern to find some way of getting along together and thereby of perpetuating the relationship and, maximally, the concern not to profit at the expense of the other. If political friendship does involve these motivations, then it seems to lead naturally into a commitment to the egalitarian liberal political order. To repeat, I do not claim that political friendship *must* involve these motivations. Perhaps in some cases it will not, and perhaps in those cases it will prove to be subversive of the liberal political order. All that my argument tries to show is that it is not implausible to regard political friendship as supportive of the liberal political order. This is sufficient to counter the strong charge that political friendship is intrinsically illiberal.

Turning now to the second concern I have identified under the heading of subversion, there is a worry that, while friendship might not be directly undermining of the liberal political order, it nevertheless provides an extremely fragile basis for political life. The fragility of friendship is particularly evident in Kant's treatment of the subject in which he finds it necessary to warn his audience of the dangers of friendship:

> We must so conduct ourselves towards a friend that there is no harm done if he should turn into an enemy. We must give him no handle against us. We ought not, of course, to assume the possibility of his becoming an enemy; any such assumption would destroy confidence between us; but it is very unwise to place ourselves in a friend's hands completely (Kant, 1991, 217).

Here Kant emphasizes the capriciousness of friendship. When friendship is not grounded in principle, or in some sort of concrete commonality, when it is basic in the sense I have described, it seems to become rather unpredictable. The fact that I am concerned for my friend today does not entail that I shall be so concerned tomorrow. We know from experience that friendships come and go and that their course can sometimes seem extremely uncertain. Friendship, therefore, is not obviously the most appropriate bond for a political community. This worry seems particularly acute where the political community in question is supposed to be that of a morally diverse and conflicted liberal society. Even supposing that it is possible for friendship to obtain at that level, it seems hard to believe that it could last. We might well fear with Kant the possibility that our political friends might one day soon become our political enemies.

In response to this concern we might begin by questioning the validity of Kant's characterization of friendship. Is it really quite as unstable as he implies? Ralph Waldo Emerson certainly thought otherwise, remarking in his 'Essay on Friendship' that 'I do not wish to treat friendships daintily, but with roughest courage. When they are real, they are not glass threads or frostwork, but the solidest thing we know' (Emerson, 1993, 44). In fact it is rather rare for one's friends suddenly to become one's enemies; certainly it is not anticipated in the normal run of events. But could the same be said of political friendship? Where the bond between us lacks the intimacy and intensity of commitment we might expect to find in a personal friendship, is it not more likely to crumble under the stresses and strains of modern political life? While Emerson felt that the closest and truest friendships could be 'the solidest thing we know', he was also careful to stress that thinner friendships are less reliable 'because we have made them a texture of wine and dreams, instead of the tough fiber of the human heart' (Emerson, 1993, 42–3). Must political friendship, once spread so thinly across the contours of a modern society, lose its solidity and wane precisely when it is needed most?

I do not think so. Again the problem here may be partly a defect of the modern classification of 'friendship' as the name of an essentially sentimental, affection-based, attachment. When we think of friendship as a form of social and political relationship, a commitment based not on fickle affection, but basic concern, it is less clear that we must necessarily think of it as being especially fragile. Political friends 'need not regard their concern for one another as affection at all. Their concern is given in what they do and how they respond to one another. There is no reason why this should be particularly unstable' (Marshall, 1998, 217). Think back to the example I gave earlier: generally speaking, we would want to help a stranger who fell over in the street, and we would feel that we had let this person down if we neglected to do so. Is it really plausible to think that this disposition to help, and the basic concern that seems to underpin it, is peculiarly unstable? In fact, it would surely be rather strange for a person who had once been concerned in this way for the weal and woe of his fellow citizens suddenly just to stop being concerned; that is not what normally happens. Our normal expectation is that the disposition to friendliness will endure (even where the affection of personal friendship has waned); typically, it does.

One might, nevertheless, still harbour the suspicion that political friendship possesses an unacceptably unpredictable character. As I suggested in the last chapter, the purposes of political friendship are a consequence of the attachment and not a structuring condition of it. Consequently, we might fear that, even though it may not collapse, the shape of the association would constantly and erratically fluctuate in a manner that could only destabilize the polity. Political stability, it might be said, requires stability of expectations, and, because political friendship is not 'pre-structured' – because its character is not determined and constrained by a prior set of shared purposes – it is intrinsically subversive of the formation of stable expectations. I think this objection is mistaken and revealingly so. My response is that it does not follow from the fact that political friendship is not pre-structured that it cannot be structured at all. We can see this in Mark Vernon's interesting discussion of 'sworn brotherhood' (Vernon, 2005, 112–14). Vernon describes the intriguing medieval practice of sworn brotherhood as 'a voluntary form of kinship based upon an exchanged promise of committed friendship' (Vernon, 2005, 113). This practice served to render friendship a semi-institutional bond. Friends would make a stable and publicly recognized commitment to one another in a manner not altogether different from marriage. The point here is that, while the friendship of sworn brothers is not pre-structured – their concern for one another is the source and not the consequence of shared purposes – their relationship is nevertheless structured. It is 'post-structured' by the formal agreement they have made, which in turn enables the parties to the relationship to form (relatively) stable expectations about the future of the attachment.

Vernon is rather sceptical about the prospect of sworn brotherhood playing much of a role in modern society. In the Middle Ages, he explains, 'civic friendship found a place because social institutions were inclusive enough to embrace it; marriage and feudal ties were inter-, over- and under-woven with bonds of friendship. This suggests, in turn, that a high doctrine of civic friendship does not enjoy much purchase today' (Vernon, 2005, 142–3). Of course there is some truth in this, but the idea of sworn brotherhood can shed some light on the possibilities for civic friendship in the context of modernity. The modern political analogue of sworn brotherhood is surely the social contract. This might seem a strange thing to suggest, because typically the device of the social contract, as it is deployed in the social contract tradition, is regarded precisely as a device for pre-structuring political relationships which, otherwise, would not obtain. We sign up to the social contract to provide stable structure to a life that would otherwise be nasty, brutish and short, and not to express an antecedent bond of friendship between us. Certainly it is true that my characterization of the social contract brings it rather closer to what we might more commonly think of as a 'covenant', an institutional commitment that is 'neither an alliance of interests nor, strictly speaking, an emotional state. Instead it is a bond of identity, as if to say: "This is part of *who I am*"' (Sacks, 2004, 178). And we might think this a rather odd way of characterizing the modern liberal social contract, but in fact, and as I have indicated in this section, it does not really seem so very far removed from what Rawls himself had in mind when he suggested that one merit of the difference principle was that it served to express the fraternity of liberal citizens.

My claim, then, is that political friendship need not be unpredictable, because it is plausible to suppose that it could constitute a semi-institutional relationship post-structured by the dictates of the liberal social contract. The idea is that political friends make a formal and enduring commitment to one another in the form of a social contract as an expression of their concern for each other. This commitment could plausibly provide a basis for the formation of stable expectations about our political life together and thus provides another, and final, counter to the charge that political friendship is intrinsically subversive of the liberal political order.

Motivation

The problem of motivation is best introduced by returning to the journey of Monsignor Quixote and Sancho in Graham Greene's novel. Having embarked on their travels, the question of their attachment to one another continues to trouble both men and soon resurfaces:

> 'Isn't "friend" going a little bit far between a Catholic priest and a Marxist?'
>
> 'You said a few hours back that we must have something in common.'
>
> 'Perhaps what we have in common is this manchegan wine, friend.' (Greene, 2000, 51).

The question I want to emphasize here is the motivational question: why should we be political friends with our moral adversaries? One might think that by characterizing the attachment of political friendship as a 'basic' attachment and as, in that sense, unconditional, there remains no motivational question to answer. Father Quixote and Sancho *just do* care about each other; there is no further story to be told here about *why* they do so.

But I do not think that quite right. To be sure, the kinds of friendships we are concerned with here are relationships which cannot plausibly be explained by appeal to the properties of the friend. They are basic. But it does not follow from that that we must or should take no interest in the task of *providing* grounds for the attachment. I might very well feel that my attachment to my friend is basic, and in that sense unconditional, and yet nevertheless feel that it is important for me to be able to articulate a plausible account of the friendship, and of how it could have come about, an account which will serve to render my devotion intelligible. Indeed, we might reasonably suppose that the best kind of friend would positively *want* to be able to provide such an account of her friendship. I might very well think that if I really cared about you, I should want to be able to explain why my commitment to you is not groundless. Of course, some people – the incurable romantics – will argue the reverse: that if I really cared about you, then there should be no question of my explaining myself and my commitment. But I do not think that most reflective people see things in that way. For most of us it is quite natural to want to be able, at least in principle, to answer the person who insists that our friendship is irrational.[3]

This is particularly striking in the case of Father Quixote and Sancho. Their friendship is certainly rather peculiar. Indeed, there appear to be good reasons for thinking that really they should not be friends at all. After all, they adhere to radically opposing moral doctrines. Consequently, there is a real question of why their association is not just a product of manchegan wine-fuelled madness and, more significantly, of why their association does not constitute an offence against their respective moral doctrines. It seems to me not ridiculous to suppose that if they really cared about each other, they would be concerned to provide answers to those questions. As it happens, of course, they are concerned to do so, and it forms one of the central themes of the novel.

Now this is not only a problem for father Quixote and Sancho; it is also a very acute problem for us. Why should we see our moral adversaries as political friends? There is a weaker and a stronger charge here. The weaker charge is just that there is something rather odd about being basically concerned for those with whom one disagrees substantially on moral matters: is it plausible to suggest that we could really be concerned for such people? The stronger charge is that in so far as we are genuinely concerned for such people, we should not be. Kukathas writes, the 'more substantial the commitments and obligations that come with membership of a political community, the more likely there is to be conflict between the demands of the political community and those of other communities to which the individual belongs. Giving political community greater importance must mean weakening other communal ties' (Kukathas, 2003, 177). On this view, it is a form of moral dysfunction or schizophrenia to be concerned for one's moral opponents and constitutes an offence against the other things for which one professes to care. In this section, I shall aim to respond to both of these charges. Before I begin, though, I want to clarify the nature of the motivational task I am setting here. I begin from the supposition that we just do regard our fellow citizens as our political friends. The motivational account is not intended as an *ex ante* rationalization of political friendship; it is not intended to convince a person who is a 'stranger' (in MacIntyre's sense which I discussed in the Introduction), to form political friendships with her fellow citizens. Rather, I hope to provide an *ex post* rationalization of political friendship, an account that a person who finds herself already involved in such relations might give to render those relations intelligible.[4]

One might think this rather disappointing; surely the real motivational difficulty concerns those who are not *already* political friends. I think this worry can be softened somewhat by recalling the considerations I presented in the Introduction: on the whole we are not strangers to one another. Political friendship is already quite widespread. The task is to consolidate and extend an attachment which already exists, not to conjure basic concern out of thin air. Of course not everybody participates in the practice of political friendship; however rare they may be, there are certainly some 'strangers' out there. But I think that such people are a political problem, and not a philosophical problem. If we expect philosophy to be able to provide a motivation for people who do not care at all about their fellow citizens to start caring, then I fear that we are going to be disappointed.

Turning, then, to the weaker charge: surely it must be a mistake to think of ourselves as basically concerned for our moral adversaries. It is a commonplace in the philosophical literature of friendship that 'like is friend to like'. The idea is central to Aristotle's account of virtue friendship. He argues that it is 'surely impossible' for a man to be the friend of one he deems bad, 'assuming that not everything is lovable but only what is good' (Aristotle, 1976, 1165b10–15). Although Aristotle is referring here specifically to personal, virtue friendship, the concern can be generalized. The political friendship of political adversaries seems, on this view, peculiar, unless, of course, it is a friendship for advantage. This, Aristotle suggests, is entirely plausible, 'because each, being eager to secure what he happens to lack himself, is prepared to give something else in return' (Aristotle, 1976, 1159b10–15). But I have suggested that the political friendship I have in mind is not advantage friendship. Political friends are genuinely concerned for one another, and there is a real question, prompted by the philosophical literature on friendship, of whether this is even possible.

There is some philosophical support for the idea that moral adversaries could be political friends. It comes from Heraclitus, though it is from Aristotle that we get the evidence for this, for he attributes to Heraclitus the view that 'opposition unites', and that 'from the different comes the fairest harmony' (Aristotle, 1976, 1155b5–10).[5] It is striking that this Heraclitean view of friendship drops out of the philosophical discourse almost immediately. Socrates expresses scepticism about the possibility of opposites uniting in friendship in Plato's *Lysis* (Plato, 1991), and Aristotle, as we have seen, also denies it. The possibility does not then resurface in the literature until much later. This absence is particularly remarkable, for in modernity, at least, the idea of opposites attracting in friendship is so commonplace that it almost has the status of a cliché. As Dean Cocking and Jeanette Kennett remark, it 'seems a matter of common observation that people who are markedly dissimilar can be very good friends' (Cocking and Kennett, 1998, 507). Almost all of us have had the experience of personal friendship with those whose moral views diverge significantly from our own, and the idea is also a common-place in our literary heritage. In the course of this book, we have already encountered the examples of George and Lennie, Don Quixote and Sancho Panza and Father Quixote and Sancho. Whilst Cocking and Kennett are right to emphasize that 'common wisdom on these matters is ambiguous' and as such is of little help to their inquiry into the nature of friendship (Cocking and Kennet, 1998, 507), it is of relevance to the question I am considering here because it reveals that in fact there is at least nothing unfamiliar in the idea of moral adversaries as friends. To be sure, none of this refutes Aristotle's claim that the unlike cannot (*really*) be friends, but I think that most of us would be extremely reluctant to endorse the implication of that claim: that Father Quixote and Sancho (and the rest) are not really friends.

So, I do not think there is anything particularly strange in the suggestion that we might, quite genuinely, regard our moral adversaries as our political friends, especially given that, when it comes to political friendship, there is no requirement that we actually like these people or that we wish to spend large amounts of our time with them. All that is being suggested is that we might be genuinely concerned (albeit rather minimally) for the well-being of those whose moral beliefs diverge from our own. The idea that this is somehow 'impossible' is surely too strong. But it seems to me that the stronger charge I mentioned above is a great deal more troubling. It is one thing to say that the political friendship of moral adversaries is *possible*, quite another to think it *desirable*. As Aristotle observes, even if such friendship were possible, 'it is not right, ... because one ought not to be a lover of what is bad, or to make oneself like a worthless person' (Aristotle, 1976, 1165b10–20). Father Quixote ought not to love Sancho and vice-versa. Father Quixote offends against his Catholic beliefs and possibly even degrades himself by associating in friendship with a Marxist. And this concern also bites politically. For example, it might be said that the socialist campaigner offends against her moral beliefs and even degrades herself by expressing genuine concern and political friendship for an economic conservative. If she were *really* devoted to the socialist cause, the objection runs, she would not associate with her adversaries in that way.

The task here is to provide a story of the motivation to political friendship with one's moral adversaries which renders the attachment consistent and congruent with one's devotion to one's moral beliefs. My use of the word 'story' here is significant. The idea is not to provide a true explanation of the origin of political friendship, but rather to articulate a 'just-so' story to be given *ex post* that may serve to render the attachment intelligible in the light of one's other, apparently conflicting, commitments. The story I plan to tell comes in two stages. In the first stage, which I shall cover fairly swiftly, I shall make the relatively modest claim that political friendship with moral adversaries need not constitute an offence against the other things for which one professes to care. In the second stage, I shall make the more ambitious claim that political friendship with moral adversaries can actually be seen to *flow from* one's commitment to the other things for which one professes to care.

First, then, we may note that there is a certain oddity in the idea that associating with, and being concerned for, one's moral adversaries must necessarily constitute an offence against one's moral beliefs. For example, is it really an offence against a person's atheism to exhibit friendship for a Christian? To insist that it is would seem to bespeak a particularly sanctimonious or over-zealous view of what it is to hold a moral belief. Clearly we can easily imagine the case of a very devout Christian insisting that her political friendship with an atheistic Marxist constituted no offence against her religion, because, as far as she is concerned, her religion does not require that she exhibit concern only for fellow Christians. It would have to be either an extremely fanatical or fragile moral doctrine that could not tolerate its holder's association with moral opponents. What I mean to emphasize here is that one does not need to be any sort of diversity-cherishing multiculturalist to feel uneasy about the suggestion that it could be a moral offence to associate with those who disagree with us.

Nevertheless, many of us might regard such association as both risky and undesirable. Even if it does not actively undermine our devotion to the other things we care about, we might nevertheless feel that there is something morally schizophrenic about the phenomenon of political friendship. But this is where my more ambitious claim comes in. I want to suggest that it would not be implausible to render one's political friendship for one's moral adversaries intelligible by appeal to one's moral beliefs. That is to say that the socialist campaigner, for example, might plausibly account for her political friendship with the economic conservative by appeal to her devotion to the socialist cause. It seems to me that there is an entirely reasonable story to be told here.

The story begins by observing that if we really care about something, then we should want it to flourish. If I really care about my best friend, I should wish her health, happiness and success. Similarly, if I really care about a moral cause – like social justice – then I should want to do what I can to further that cause. This feature of caring may seem to be the source of our motivational difficulties: if I want to further the socialist cause, what am I doing fraternizing with the 'enemy'? But, in fact, I want to suggest that it provides the key to answering the motivational challenge. The story goes like this. I care about the socialist cause and I want it to flourish. This provides me with reason to want to convince those who do not care for the socialist cause to change their minds, since my socialist cause will flourish best in a world in which nobody disputes its value. So, my concern for socialism leads me into the political sphere and into the collective activity of political argument and debate with my moral opponents. In other words, I begin to work with my political opponents within the common institutional framework of the modern democratic society. Over time, and as Stuart Hampshire has observed, it is not implausible to suppose that, because we share this common institutional life and work together in this way, we will 'naturally come to share certain professional attitudes and customs, and a common professional morality' (Hampshire, 1999, 48–9). We could very plausibly come to develop a measure of institutional respect and non-instrumental concern for our moral adversaries. We could become political friends.

One might hesitate here. The story I have told may seem rather too instrumental. It may be thought to imply that we are only friends with our moral adversaries because we want to 'convert' them to our way of thinking. But that is not what I mean to suggest. It is easier to see this if we tell the story backwards. My suggestion is that we begin from a person who is already *non-instrumentally* concerned for her moral adversary. The task is to explain how this relationship could plausibly have come about. The first stage of the answer suggests that one might come to be non-instrumentally concerned for one's moral opponent by sharing a life with her under common institutions. But then we might ask why a person should wish to share an institutional life with his moral adversary in the first place. The second stage of the answer suggests that moral adversaries might wish to share a life under common institutions because they wanted to convert each other, to show each other the error of their respective ways. In other words, then, the story begins by appealing to the instrumental value of associating with one's moral adversaries, but suggests a way in which one's instrumental concern could evolve into non-instrumental concern.

Among those who share an institutional life, we might expect to detect the emergence of what Hampshire calls 'moral cross-currents' (Hampshire, 1999, 49). I will find myself substantially committed to my moral friends and my socialist cause yet I will also find myself procedurally committed to my political friends and our shared institutional life. It is at this point that the motivational worry arises: these 'moral cross-currents' are perverse and corrupt; we should not be concerned for our moral adversaries. But on the story I have told, it is now possible to answer this motivational challenge. The answer goes like this: I find myself in relations of political friendship with my moral adversaries precisely because I am devoted to the socialist cause. It was in the course of trying to further that cause that I formed these relationships and, consequently, it would be an offence against the socialist cause for me to seek now to extricate myself by resigning from the public activity in which I am involved. On this view, then, political friendship is justified *in the name* of our substantial moral beliefs.

Note that this is a variation on a theme quite prevalent in the literature on 'dirty hands' in public life. It is thought that sometimes, and quite commonly in politics, it can be morally necessary to behave in a morally distasteful way. From the perspective of my substantial socialist morality, we might very well regard my political friendship with economic conservatives as being both morally distasteful and yet also morally necessary. A parallel, though rather extreme case, is suggested by Martin Hollis when he discusses 'those German judges appointed under the Weimar Republic, who found themselves still in office under the Nazis and set to administer growingly anti-Semitic laws.' He observes that some 'resigned but others, reckoning that they would merely be replaced by ardent Nazis, stayed on, grimly trying to do some slight good' (Hollis, 1996c, 143). The point here is not to suggest that those who stayed on necessarily did the right thing, but rather to emphasize that in no way did their staying on constitute any sort of offence against their substantial moral beliefs. On the contrary, they behaved as they did out of *devotion* to their moral beliefs.

Returning, then, to the liberal political community of friends, my suggestion is that a person could quite reasonably hold that she was a political friend to her moral adversaries just because she cared so much about the moral ideals to which she was devoted. To repeat, I am not suggesting that this is necessarily a *true* story of the formation of political friendship. As I argued in the last chapter, the formation of this sort of basic attachment is necessarily mysterious. But I am suggesting that the story I have articulated provides a plausible *ex post* rationalization of a political relationship that may, on the face of it, seem rather implausible or even corrupt. The story I have told has one final intriguing implication: it suggests that conflict might in fact be *necessary* for political community. I have argued that the only way in which we can plausibly render political friendship intelligible is by appeal to a motivational story to which discord is central. It is only because they fundamentally diverge on moral matters that we are able to make sense of the political friendship between the socialist and the economic conservative. If they did not disagree so passionately, it would be harder to explain why they might have wanted to share an institutional life in the public sphere in the first place. Political friends defend their attachment to one another by appeal to the fact that they disagree. Here, then, is a striking thought: one of the most important sources of social unity in a liberal society is provided by conflict.

Conclusion: Community and conflict

In this chapter, I have sought to show that, far from being an absurdly utopian aspiration, the idea that the liberal community could be a community of political friends is an entirely realistic notion, one that is in fact far less utopian than the prevailing accounts of liberal community which suppose that we might somehow come to share with our fellow citizens a comprehensive conception of the liberal good or an ethically substantive national identity. I have defended this claim, first, by suggesting that it is not unrealistic, and is, in fact, quite commonplace, for people to be genuinely and basically concerned for the other members of their society even though they may not know or like them. Secondly, I have denied the accusation that being concerned in this way is somehow intrinsically subversive of the liberal order. On the contrary, I have argued that the liberal social contract can plausibly be seen as an *expression* of political friendship. Finally, I have argued that political friendship does not imply any sort of moral schizophrenia on the part of the agent. Rather, the formation of such friendship can be seen as an *expression* of our devotion to the things we care about.

I began this book by noting the widespread conviction that conflict is undermining of community, that it is the understandings we share that make us into a community and that modern society is nothing but a collection of strangers, each pursuing his own interests under minimal constraints. I have sought to challenge and correct this impression. First, I questioned the characterization of our societies as estranged and disputed the conventional vocabulary of communal association. I examined some of the shapes a shared life might take and, by appeal to journey narratives of escape and quest, I contended that conflict need not constitute a barrier to community. It is possible for liberal political community to survive in conditions of conflict if we conceive of that community as an association of political friends who share in the resistance of common ills and travel together out of basic concern one for another. My final contention in this chapter has been altogether stronger and aims to leave an impression diametrically opposed to that with which we began. I have sought to tell a story of the passage into community as prompted not by the understandings we share, but by those we do not. Here is an image of liberal political community not merely surviving, but flourishing in conditions of conflict: a 'back-turning harmony', a labour of love.[6]

Notes

Introduction: Strangers

1 Needless to say, my treatment of the sociological literature here is extremely brief. I do not intend to provide anything like a comprehensive survey of the literature, merely to draw attention to the fact that the vision of modern society as a collection of strangers is one with considerable force.
2 This statistic is derived from surveys in which people were asked whether or not other people could be trusted.
3 The question was directed towards 3800 British donors.

Chapter 1   Why Liberal Community Matters

1 Though it is worth noting that Mason deploys this expression in a slightly different context: he uses the expression to denote the experience of those bound by a strong sense of common nationality.
2 In fact, Mason goes rather further than this and suggests that identification need not even be moral. As he puts it, 'some may regard these institutions as merely instrumentally valuable because they promote their interests' (Mason, 2000, 138). It seems to me, however, that by making his conception of community as inclusive as this, Mason risks collapsing his own distinction between community and 'mere society', the latter of which is supposed to describe purely instrumental associations.
3 There is of course a further question here of why stability should matter. Liberals tend not to pursue this question, beginning instead from the assumption that it just does matter, and I shall not pursue the question here. Though, for the contrasting view that in fact seems to me rather plausible, see Stuart Hampshire's review of *Political Liberalism* (Hampshire, 1993).
4 Though it is worth noting that not all liberals would agree with Rawls's perspective here. Brian Barry, for example, seems fairly content to coerce those unable freely to identify themselves with the requirements of liberal justice (Barry, 1995, 64).
5 It may be worth noting here that 'community' here is variously rendered as 'city' and as 'state' by other translators. I do not think that this undermines the general claim I am making – that Plato supposes that the ideal political constitution will be characterized by a very high degree of consensus.
6 See also Yack, 1993, 29–30.
7 See Nussbaum, 2001, 343–72.

Chapter 2   The Shape of a Shared Life

1 See also MacIntyre, 1985, 212–13.
2 Of course, the Exodus is a not fictional story in any ordinary sense. My point here is rather that it corresponds to a journey pattern that has become commonplace in fictional narratives.
3 Of course there are senses in which the author of fiction aspires to truthfulness. It is often thought to be important that a fictional narrative *feels* plausible or authentic. I shall return to this point in a moment.

Chapter 3   Community as Pilgrimage

1 My discussion of Bunyan's narrative here has been influenced by Stewart Sutherland's British Academy Isaiah Berlin lecture, 'Nomad's Progress'. An audio recording of the lecture is available on the British Academy website (http://britac.studyserve.com/home/Lecture.asp?ContentContainerID=96 accessed 27/04/05 at 1400). Other examples of pilgrimage narratives are provided by Chaucer's *The Canterbury Tales*, which I shall discuss shortly, and also William Langland's *Piers The Ploughman* (Langland, 1966).
2 Stewart Sutherland draws this distinction between the pilgrim and the tourist. See Chapter 3, note 1.
3 One should not be misled by my use of 'sacred' and 'trivial' here. I do not mean to suggest that taking photographs of pretty mosques is necessarily trivial. If a person regarded photographing pretty mosques in Mecca as a central constituent of her practical identity, then we might meaningfully speak of such an activity as sacred (or 'higher') for her and, as such, the proper object of a pilgrimage for her.
4 Bernard Yack's description of the composition of Aristotelian community suggests a colourful assortment of characters not so very far removed from the Canterbury pilgrims: 'Men and women, farmers and shoemakers, sailors and passengers, aristocratic and peasant families – such are the members of Aristotelian communities' (Yack, 1993, 30).
5 It is instructive to compare Macedo's 'California dream', with the perspective of Yael Tamir when she writes that 'a post-national age in which national differences are obliterated and all share in one shallow universal culture, watch soap operas and CNN, eat McDonalds, drink Coca-Cola, and take the children to the local Disneyworld, is more a nightmare than a utopian vision' (Tamir, 1993, 166–7).
6 See, for example, the *Guardian* article, 'I'm happy my child is deaf' (Ridgeway, 2002).
7 Of course we might feel that this last is really no hardship. If we give up on the 'pre-scripting' requirement, the shared life of the community will look rather less like a pilgrimage and more like the kind of 'quest' that I shall discuss in Chapter 5.

Chapter 4 Community as Escape

1 Other advocates of something like this position include John Gray (Gray, 2001); Stuart Hampshire (Hampshire, 1999); and Bernard Williams (Williams, 2005).
2 This contrast is developed by MacIntyre (MacIntyre, 1999, 1–9).

Chapter 5 Community as Quest

1 Here we might note a contrast with what Janis Stout characterizes as journeys of 'home-founding' (Stout, 1983, 41–64). The Joad family, in Steinbeck's *Grapes of Wrath*, head out West precisely in order to get out West and to begin a new life. The same can be said of the Ingalls family in *Little House on The Prairie*. For Sal Paradise and his companions, the nature of the journey is quite different.

Chapter 6 On Companionship

1 My formulation here is informed by Martin Hollis's article, 'Friends, Romans and Consumers' (Hollis, 1996a, 150–69).
2 The argument I develop in this section is a condensed and somewhat altered version of an argument I have developed elsewhere in a rather different context (Edyvane, 2003).
3 Though note that this is not to say that there is nothing crazy about Don Quixote. I think that would be a difficult claim to sustain.

Chapter 7 Political Friendship

1 I borrow this term from Sandra Marshall (Marshall, 1998, 216).
2 There is also considerable dispute as to which kind of friendship Aristotle regarded as providing the most appropriate characterization of the political bond. For example, Horst Hutter, among others, suggests that Aristotelian political friendship is a relatively intimate bond (Hutter, 1978, 116). Bernard Yack, by contrast argues persuasively that Aristotle conceived of political friendship as a 'lukewarm' attachment of advantage friendship (Yack, 1993, 109–27).
3 This is a condensed version of an argument I have given elsewhere (Edyvane, 2003).
4 My formulation of these points is influenced by Martin Hollis's discussion of 'Honour Among Thieves' (Hollis, 1996b).
5 The corresponding fragment in Heraclitus is number 8 (Diels' ordering). The quotations are not thought to be exact, though see also fragments 51 and 80 (Heraclitus, 1979).
6 The quotation here is from Heraclitus, fragment 51 (Heraclitus, 1979).

References

Adams, R. 1974, *Watership Down* (Harmondsworth: Penguin).

Allen, J. 2001, 'The Place of Negative Morality in Political Theory', *Political Theory* 29: 337–63.

Anderson, B. 1991, *Imagined Communities: Reflections on the Origin and Spread of Nationalism* (London: Verso).

Arblaster, A. 1984, *The Rise and Decline of Western Liberalism* (Oxford: Blackwell).

Aristotle, 1976, *Ethics*, trans. J.A.K. Thomson (London: Penguin).

Aristotle, 1984, *The Politics*, trans. B. Jowett (Cambridge: Cambridge University Press).

Baier, A. 1994, 'Trust and Antitrust' in her *Moral Prejudices: Essays on Ethics* (Cambridge, Mass.: Harvard University Press).

Barry, B. 1989, 'The Continuing Relevance of Socialism' in R. Skidelsky (ed.), *Thatcherism* (Oxford: Blackwell, 1989), pp. 143–58.

Barry, B. 1995, *Justice as Impartiality* (Oxford: Oxford University Press).

Barry, B. 1996, 'Does society exist? The case for socialism' in P. King (ed.), *Socialism and The Common Good: New Fabian Essays* (London: Frank Cass), pp. 115–43.

Barry, B. 2001, *Culture and Equality: An Egalitarian Critique of Multiculturalism* (Cambridge: Polity).

Bellah, R. *et al.* 1985, *Habits of the Heart: Middle America Observed* (London: Hutchinson).

Berman, M. 1983, *All That Is Solid Melts Into Air* (London: Verso).

Bernstein, M. 1985, 'Love, Particularity, and Selfhood', *Southern Journal of Philosophy* 23/3: 287–93.

Bunyan, J. 1984, *The Pilgrim's Progress* (Oxford: Oxford University Press).

Calder, A. 1969, *The People's War* (London: Pimlico).

Cavafy, C.P. 1976, 'Ithaca' in his *The Complete Poems of Cavafy*, R. Dalven trans. (San Diego: Harcourt Brace & Co.).

Cervantes, M. 2005, *Don Quixote*, E. Grossman trans. (London: Vintage).

Chaucer, G. 1985, *The Canterbury Tales*, trans. D. Wright (Oxford: Oxford University Press).

Cocking, D. and Kennett, J. 1998, 'Friendship and the Self', *Ethics* 108/3: 502–27.

Delaney, N. 1996, 'Romantic Love and Loving Commitment: Articulating a Modern Ideal', *American Philosophical Quarterly* 33/4: 339–56.

Douglass, F. 1999, *Narrative of the Life of Frederick Douglass, An American Slave* (Oxford: Oxford University Press).

Dreben, B. 2003, 'On Rawls and Political Liberalism' in S. Freeman (ed.), *The Cambridge Companion to Rawls* (Cambridge: Cambridge University Press), pp. 316–46.

Dworkin, R. 2000, *Sovereign Virtue: The Theory and Practice of Equality* (Cambridge, Mass.: Harvard University Press).

Edwards, P. 1980, 'The Journey in *The Pilgrim's Progress*' in V. Newey (ed.), *The Pilgrim's Progress: Critical and Historical Views* (Liverpool: Liverpool University Press).

Edyvane, D. 2003, 'Against Unconditional Love', *Journal of Applied Philosophy* 20/1: 59–75.

Emerson, R. 'Friendship' in *Self-Reliance and Other Essays* (New York: Dover), pp. 39–50.

Frankfurt, H. 2004, *The Reasons of Love* (Princeton: Princeton University Press).

Frazer, E. 1999, *The Problems of Communitarian Politics: Unity and Conflict* (Oxford: Oxford University Press).

Galston, W. 1991, *Liberal Purposes: Goods, Virtues, and Diversity in the Liberal State* (Cambridge: Cambridge University Press).

Galston, W. 2002, *Liberal Pluralism: The Implications of Value Pluralism for Political Theory and Practice* (Cambridge: Cambridge University Press).

Gould, C. 2004, *Globalizing Democracy and Human Rights* (Cambridge: Cambridge University Press).

Gray, J. 2001, 'Two Liberalisms of Fear', *Hedgehog Review* 2.

Greene, G. 2000, *Monsignor Quixote* (London: Vintage).

Hampshire, S. 1983, *Morality and Conflict* (Oxford: Blackwell).

Hampshire, S. 1989, *Innocence and Experience* (London: Penguin).

Hampshire, S. 1993, 'Liberalism: The New Twist', *New York Review of Books*, August 12, 1993, pp. 43–7.

Hampshire, S. 1999, *Justice is Conflict* (London: Duckworth).

Heraclitus, 1979, 'The Fragments' in C. Kahn ed. and trans, *The art and thought of Heraclitus: An edition of the fragments with translation and commentary* (Cambridge: Cambridge University Press).

Hollis, M. 1996a, 'Friends, Romans and Consumers' in his *Reason in Action* (Cambridge: Cambridge University Press), pp. 150–69.

Hollis, M. 1996b, 'Honour Among Thieves' in his *Reason in Action* (Cambridge: Cambridge University Press), pp. 109–30.

Hollis, M. 1996c, 'Dirty Hands' in his *Reason in Action* (Cambridge: Cambridge University Press), pp. 131–49.

Hollis, M. 1998, *Trust Within Reason* (Cambridge: Cambridge University Press).

Horton J. 1996, 'Life, Literature and Ethical Theory: Martha Nussbaum on the role of the literary imagination in ethical thought' in J. Horton and A. Baumeister (eds), *Literature and the Political Imagination* (London: Routledge), pp. 70–97.

Hutter, 1978, *Politics as Friendship: The origins of classical notions of politics in the theory and practice of friendship* (Waterloo, Ontario: Wilfrid Laurier University Press).

Ignatieff, M. 1984, *The Needs of Strangers* (London: Hogarth Press).

Jerome, J.K. 1957, *Three Men in a Boat* (London: Penguin).

Kahane, D. 1999, 'Diversity, Solidarity and Civic Friendship', *Journal of Political Philosophy* 7/3: 267–86.

Kant, I. 1991, 'Lecture on Friendship' in M. Pakaluk (ed.), *Other Selves: Philosophers on Friendship* (Indianapolis: Hackett), pp. 210–17.

Keller, S. 2000, 'How do I Love Thee? Let me Count the Properties', *American Philosophical Quarterly* 37/2: 163–73.

Kerouac, J. 1991, *On The Road* (London: Penguin).

Kukathas, C. 2003, *The Liberal Archipelago* (Oxford: Oxford University Press).

Kymlicka, W. 1996, *Multicultural Citizenship* (Oxford: Oxford University Press).

Langland, W. 1966, *Piers The Ploughman* (Harmondsworth: Penguin).

Larmore, C. 2003, 'Public Reason' in S. Freeman (ed.), *The Cambridge Companion to Rawls* (Cambridge: Cambridge University Press), pp. 368–93.

Levine, M. 1999, 'Loving Individuals for Their Properties Or, What Was the Colour of Yeats's Mother's Hair?', *Iyyun, The Jerusalem Philosophical Quarterly* 48: 251–67.

Macedo, S. 1990, *Liberal Virtues: Citizenship, Virtue, and Community in Liberal Constitutionalism* (Oxford: Oxford University Press).

MacIntyre, A. 1985, *After Virtue: A Study in Moral Theory*.

MacIntyre, A. 1999, *Dependent Rational Animals: Why Human Beings Need The Virtues* (London: Duckworth).

Malory, T. 1998, *Le Morte Darthur* (Oxford: Oxford University Press).

Marshall, S. 1998, 'The Community of Friends' in E.A. Christodoulidis (ed.), *Communitarianism and Citizenship* (Aldershot: Ashgate), pp. 208–19.

Mason, A. 2000, *Community, Solidarity and Belonging: Levels of Community and their Normative Significance* (Cambridge: Cambridge University Press).

Matarasso, P.M. (trans). 1969, *The Quest of the Holy Grail* (London: Penguin).

Mendus, S. 1996, '"What of soul was left, I wonder?" The narrative self in political philosophy' in J. Horton and A. Baumeister (eds), *Literature and the Political Imagination* (London: Routledge), pp. 53–69.

Mendus, S. 2001, 'Marital Faithfulness' in her *Feminism and Emotion: Readings in Moral and Political Philosophy* (Houndmills: Macmillan), pp. 69–80.

Mendus, S. 2002, *Impartiality in Moral and Political Philosophy* (Oxford: Oxford University Press).

Miller, D. 1989, 'In What Sense Must Socialism be Communitarian?', *Social Philosophy and Policy* 6/2: 51–73.

Miller, D. 1995, *On Nationality* (Oxford: Oxford University Press).

Montaigne, M. 1991, 'Of Friendship' in M. Pakaluk (ed.), *Other Selves: Philosophers on Friendship* (Indianapolis: Hackett), pp. 187–99.

Moon, J.D. 1993, *Constructing Community: Moral Pluralism and Tragic Conflicts* (Princeton: Princeton University Press).

Murdoch, I. 1997a, 'Against Dryness' in P. Conradi (ed.), *Existentialists and Mystics: Writings on Philosophy and Literature* (London: Chatto and Windus), pp. 287–95.

Murdoch, I. 1997b, 'Literature and Philosophy: A Conversation with Bryan Magee' in P. Conradi (ed.), *Existentialists and Mystics: Writings on Philosophy and Literature* (London: Chatto and Windus), pp. 3–30.

Musil, R. 1995, *The Man Without Qualities*, S. Wilkins and B. Pike trans. (London: Picador).

Nussbaum, M. 2001, *The Fragility of Goodness: Luck and Ethics in Greek Tragedy and Philosophy* (Cambridge: Cambridge University Press).

Oakeshott, M. 1975, *On Human Conduct* (Oxford: Oxford University Press).

Phillips, D.Z. 1982, *Through a darkening glass: philosophy, literature, and cultural change* (Oxford: Blackwell).

Plato, 1993, *Republic*, R. Waterfield trans. (Oxford: Oxford University Press).

Putnam, R.D. 2000, *Bowling Alone: The Collapse and Revival of American Community* (New York: Simon & Schuster).

Rawls, J. 1971, *A Theory of Justice* (Oxford: Oxford University Press).

Rawls, J. 1996, *Political Liberalism* (New York: Columbia University Press).

Rawls, J. 1999, *A Theory of Justice, revised edition* (Oxford: Oxford University Press).

Rawls, J. 1999, *Collected Papers*, S. Freeman (ed.) (Cambridge, Mass.: Harvard University Press).

Raz, J. 2001, *Value, Respect and Attachment* (Cambridge: Cambridge University Press).

Ridgeway, S. 2002, 'I'm happy my child is deaf', M. Mills (interviewer), *The Guardian*, 9 April.

Sacks, J. 2004, 'Political Society, Civil Society' in J. Haldane (ed.), *Values, Education and the Human World* (Exeter: Imprint Academic), pp. 173–81.

Saint-Exupery, A. 2002, *The Little Prince* (London: Egmont).

Sandel, M. 1982, *Liberalism and the Limits of Justice* (Cambridge: Cambridge University Press).

Scheffler, S. 2006, 'Is Terrorism Morally Distinctive?', *Journal of Political Philosophy* 14/1: 1–17.

Shakespeare, W. 1975, *King Lear*, P. Edwards (ed.) (London: Macmillan).

Shklar, J. 1989, 'The Liberalism of Fear' in N. Rosenblum (ed.), *Liberalism and The Moral Life* (Cambridge, Mass.: Harvard University Press), pp. 21–38.

Steinbeck, J. 1995, *Of Mice and Men* (London: Arrow).

Stout, Janis. 1983, *The Journey Narrative in American Literature: Patterns and Departures* (Connecticut: Greenwood Press).

Stout, Jeffrey. 2001, *Ethics After Babel: The Languages of Morals and Their Discontents* (Princeton: Princeton University Press).

Strawson, G. 2004, 'Against Narrativity', *Ratio* 17/4: 428–52.

Tamir, Y. 1993, *Liberal Nationalism* (Princeton: Princeton University Press).

Taylor, C. 2004, *Modern Social Imaginaries* (Durham, N.C.: Duke University Press).

Titmuss, R.M. 1970, *The Gift Relationship: From Human Blood to Social Policy* (London: George Allen & Unwin).

Tronto, J.C. 1993, *Moral Boundaries: A Political Argument for an Ethic of Care* (New York: Routledge).

Updike, J. 1961, *Rabbit, Run* (London: Andre Deutsch).

Vernon, M. 2005, *The Philosophy of Friendship* (Houndmills: Palgrave Macmillan).

Walzer, M. 1985, *Exodus and Revolution* (New York: Basic Books).

Walzer, M. 1996, 'On Negative Politics' in B. Yack (ed.), *Liberalism Without Illusions: Essays on Liberal Theory and the Political Vision of Judith N. Shklar* (Chicago: University of Chicago Press).

Weinstock, D. 1999, 'Building Trust in Divided Societies', *Journal of Political Philosophy* 7/3: 287–307.

Whitman, W. 1990, *Leaves of Grass* (Oxford: Oxford University Press).

Wiggins, D. 1987, 'Truth, Invention, and the Meaning of Life' in his *Needs, Values, Truth: Essays in the Philosophy of Value* (Oxford: Blackwell), pp. 87–137.

Williams, B. 1983, *Moral Luck* (Cambridge: Cambridge University Press).

Williams, B. 2002, *Truth and Truthfulness: An Essay in Genealogy* (Princeton: Princeton University Press).

Williams, B. 2005, 'The Liberalism of Fear' in G. Hawthorn (ed.), *In the Beginning was the Deed: Realism and Moralism in Political Argument* (Princeton: Princeton University Press), pp. 52–61.

Yack, B. 1993, *The Problems of a Political Animal: Community, Justice, and Conflict in Aristotelian Political Thought* (Berkeley: University of California Press).

Young, I.M. 1990, *Justice and the Politics of Difference* (Princeton: Princeton University Press).

Zumthor, P. 1994, 'The Medieval Travel Narrative', trans. C. Peebles, *New Literary History* 25/4: 809–24.

Index